Personal, Social and Emotional Development in the Early Years Foundation Stage

Using the clear and accessible material in this book practitioners will be guided through the process of helping children develop an understanding of themselves; to help them gain independence and to become excited and motivated about their learning. Practical examples and ideas are linked to the practice guidance to ensure that practitioners feel confident in their ability to support and develop children's emotional well-being and social skills as well as develop their own knowledge and understanding of this important aspect of the EYFS.

Sue Sheppy is an independent Early Years educational consultant and has written extensively for the *Nursery World* magazine.

Practical Guidance in the EYFS
Series Editor: Sandy Green

The *Practical Guidance in the EYFS* series will assist practitioners in the smooth and successful implementation of the Early Years Foundation Stage.

Each book gives clear and detailed explanations of each aspect of learning and development and encourages readers to consider each area within its broadest context to expand and develop their own knowledge and good practice.

Practical ideas and activities for all age groups are offered along with a wealth of expertise of how elements from the practice guidance can be implemented within all early years' settings. The books include suggestions for the innovative use of everyday resources, popular books and stories.

Titles in this series include:

Personal, Social and Emotional Development in the Early Years Foundation Stage
Sue Sheppy

Communication, Language and Literacy in the Early Years Foundation Stage
Helen Bradford

Knowledge and Understanding of the World in the Early Years Foundation Stage
Stella Louis

Creative Development in the Early Years Foundation Stage
Pamela May

Problem Solving, Reasoning and Numeracy in the Early Years Foundation Stage
Anita M. Hughes

Physical Development in the Early Years Foundation Stage
Angela D. Nurse

Planning for the Early Years Foundation Stage
Sandra Smidt

Personal, Social and Emotional Development in the Early Years Foundation Stage

Sue Sheppy

Routledge
Taylor & Francis Group

LONDON AND NEW YORK

First published 2009
by Routledge
2 Park Square, Milton Park, Abingdon, Oxon OX14 4RN

Simultaneously published in the USA and Canada
by Routledge
270 Madison Avenue, New York, NY 10016

Routledge is an imprint of the Taylor & Francis Group, an informa business

© 2009 Susan Sheppy

Typeset in Optima by
Taylor & Francis Books
Printed and bound in Great Britain by
TJ International Ltd, Padstow, Cornwall

British Library Cataloguing in Publication Data
A catalogue record for this book is available from the British Library

Library of Congress Cataloging in Publication Data
Sheppy, Sue.
  Personal, social and emotional development in the early years foundation
  stage / Sue Sheppy.
     p. cm. – (Practical guidance in the EYFS)
  1. Child development. 2. Early childhood education. I. Title.
  LB1117.S44 2008
372.21–dc22   2008022093

ISBN 978-0-415-47838-0 (hbk)
ISBN 978-0-415-47180-0 (pbk)

To Samuel Jonathan Williams
who is seeing the world for the first time
and reminding me again of all its fascinations

Contents

Acknowledgements   ix

Introduction   1
Theoretical basis   4
Personal development   6
Social development   8
Emotional development   10
The adult perspective   12
What are Persona Dolls?   13
Why story?   14

1   Dispositions and attitudes: stories and activities   18
From birth–20 months   18
From 16–36 months   24
From 30–60+ months   30
Persona Doll story   46
The EYFS principles   49

2   Self-confidence and self-esteem: stories and activities   51
From birth–20 months   51
From 16–36 months   56
From 30–60+ months   61
Persona Doll story   70
The EYFS principles   74

3   Making relationships: stories and activities   75
From birth–20 months   75
From 16–36 months   80
From 30–60+ months   85
Persona Doll story   96
The EYFS principles   98

4   Behaviour and self-control: stories and activities   100
From birth–20 months   100
From 16–36 months   104
From 30–60+ months   113
Persona Doll story   122
The EYFS principles   125

5   Self-care: stories and activities   127
From birth–20 months   127
From 16–36 months   132
From 30–60+ months   140
Persona Doll story   148
The EYFS principles   151

6   Sense of community: stories and activities   153
From birth–20 months   153
From 16–36 months   159
From 30–60+ months   164
Persona Doll story   173
The EYFS principles   176

Further recommended reading   178

Acknowledgements

My special thanks to Babette Brown for introducing me to the world of Persona Dolls and to all my colleagues who share the work of countering discrimination and promoting the celebration of our similarities and differences.

Thanks, also, to my husband, Paul, for his unwavering support and encouragement.

Introduction

The Early Years Foundation Stage (EYFS) is a central part of the childcare strategy 'Choice for Parents, the Best Start for Children', and the Childcare Act (2006). The Act provides the context for the delivery of the EYFS, which will be mandatory from September 2008 for all schools and Early Years providers in Ofsted-registered settings attended by young children from birth to the end of the academic year in which they turn five.

The aim of the EYFS framework is to help young children achieve the five 'Every Child Matters' outcomes of staying safe, being healthy, enjoying and achieving, making a positive contribution and achieving economic well-being. It has laid down an enhanced curriculum with the intention of providing children with the best possible start in life with schools, parents and outside agencies working in partnership. Practitioners are being challenged to take greater account of child-development matters, to make observations, to plan and resource their settings in order to become even more effective in their practice. To do this, they will need to generate interesting projects for the children to explore and provide a secure, safe and stimulating environment for those in their care. This book will help practitioners to provide learning opportunities for the children which are relevant, realistic and challenging so that the unique needs of *all* the children can be met, enabling them to achieve their full potential. A child's personal, social and emotional development is fundamental to a life that makes a positive contribution. It cuts across all of the EYFS guiding themes and has implications for inclusion and for respect for oneself and for others, regardless of ethnicity, culture, religion, home language, family background, learning difficulties, gender, disabilities or talents. Children's self-image is vital to their ability to thrive in every area of their lives. As a general principle, they need to feel good about themselves if they are to cope successfully with their feelings, relate to others with respect and understanding and reach out in friendship. This book will provide a wealth of resources, including ideas for home links, which will foster positive relationships, provide enabling environments and support the children's learning and development. Practitioners who are responsible for the nurturing of young children in their settings are conscientious but busy people. This book will provide practical support for the development of the children in their care personally, socially and emotionally.

Alongside the *Statutory Framework* (DfES 2007a), the Department for Education and Skills has provided information and advice for practitioners in the form of the *Practice Guidance* (DfES 2007b). There are six areas covered by the early learning goals and educational programmes. This book supports practitioners in the element that deals with the personal, social and emotional development of children. Such development thrives in an ethos where the children are:

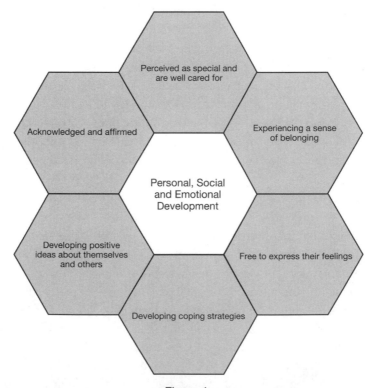

Figure 1
What Personal, Social and Emotional Development means for children
Source: DfES 2007b

It will be an invaluable resource for all those who work with young children providing them with:

- a theoretical framework in which to reflect on their own attitudes;
- additional ideas and activities for the practical implementation of this new legislation primarily through the medium of story.

In the light of the new legislation, providers have a duty to ensure that their Early Years provision complies with the learning and development requirements set out in the Statutory Framework. There are four principles that guide their work and these are grouped into the four themes of:

1   a unique child;
2   positive relationships;
3   enabling environments;
4   learning and development.

This book has used the main headings from the *Practice Guidance* and has kept as close as possible to its format. The activities are closely linked to the EYFS curriculum so that learning outcomes can be easily monitored and evaluated. They will provide key vocabulary and suggest key questions. The book follows the series format and includes a substantial summary of all relevant theories at the beginning; the focus is on research into the personal, social and emotional development of young children. It provides ideas and activities to support development throughout the EYFS, making links to the Early Learning Goals as appropriate and including ideas for relevant books and resources. The chapter headings follow the sections of learning and development set out in the *Practice Guidance* (see Figure 2). Each chapter relates to the full age range and incorporates the Early Learning Goals (see Figure 3).

Each developmental aspect has one main story allocated across the age range, as appropriate, recognising the fact that children do not follow a linear pattern of development. Also, practitioners are given a wide range of alternative titles, as in this area it is important that the storyteller feels comfortable with the way the issues are being explored. Some of these stories are from published sources while others are created around issues using intermediaries such as Persona Dolls (Brown 2001, 2008). Each story provides the basis for a number of activities and a list of additional resources.

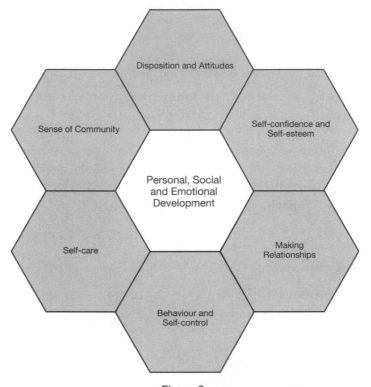

Figure 2
Areas of learning and development for Personal, Social and Emotional Development
Source: DfES 2007b

All of this is closely related to the other three categories in the learning and development sections in the *Practice Guidance,* where practitioners are exhorted to look, listen and note, to be effective in their practice and to scrutinise the appropriateness of their planning and resourcing. Each chapter will build on established good practice, ask key questions and support practitioners in extending their children's personal, social and emotional literacy.

Theoretical basis

Our basic emotions have developed to cope with our need to survive. Early human beings learnt when to stay and fight and when to run away; this was crucial for their continued existence. What was also fundamental was the need to reproduce, and this involved the nurture of each other, in particular of the young. Long (2005) identifies six basic emotions that we are born with:

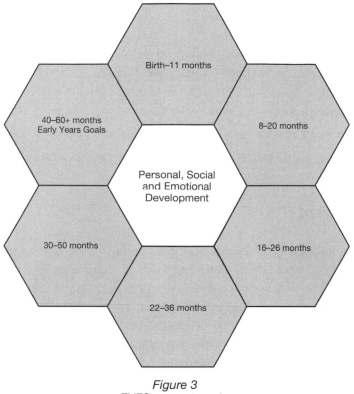

Figure 3
EYFS age categories
Source: DfES 2007b

fear, joy, surprise, anger, disgust and curiosity. While most researchers across cultures would agree with this list, many would include sadness instead of curiosity, which loads the balance on the negative side, especially as the difference between the facial expression of surprise and fear is often minimal (Ekman 2003). Long, however, contends that the negative emotions of fear, anger and disgust help to motivate us to avoid dangers, while the positive ones of joy, surprise and curiosity encourage us to explore our environment. This is undoubtedly too simplistic, as anger, for example, can positively motivate people to challenge injustice, and curiosity can lead them into situations of great danger. However, these are without question basic primary emotions that direct our behaviour right from the start and, at best, enable us to begin to experience a spiritual dimension to our lives as we relate to the world with awe and wonder. The way these emotions are managed has profound consequences for the personal, social and emotional development of the child.

Personal development

Personal development is about a child's developing confidence and Dowling (2005: 2) identifies three closely linked factors that have a direct bearing on this:

1   self-concept (becoming aware of oneself);
2   self-esteem (developing a view of oneself, either positive or negative);
3   self-knowledge (getting to know one's strengths and weaknesses).

Self-concept

At birth, babies, ideally, experience attachment to a key person who feeds them and holds them close, firmly and tenderly, thus caring for their comfort and needs. As the child develops, she needs to begin to separate herself from the primary caregiver and to develop a sense of self. This separation is frequently a time of anxiety for the child, but if this process is supported by a caring adult, then by 18 months, the child is beginning to recognise herself as a unique individual with her own identity. In the pre-school years, other people will contribute to her self-concept as she sees herself through the eyes of a wider group of people, and, as Dowling (2005: 3) says, she will begin to 'adapt her behaviour to fit this picture and learn to behave in character'.

Self-esteem

This is concerned with value judgements about ourselves. As the child develops, he receives messages all the time about his worth as a person, even from the earliest days. His level of self-esteem will depend on whether his needs are met and how he is nurtured. Perhaps his needs are gratified, but begrudgingly, as a last resort, or conversely he may be made to feel that he is precious, someone important, spoken to encouragingly, loved. By the age of three, children are beginning to make judgements based on the messages they have received from the behaviour of the adults around them. It begins to affect the way they behave, and it is those closest to the child who will maintain the strongest influence. By the end of the Foundation Stage, children will have established a clear idea of their own worth as an individual, although this will always depend to some extent on the context in which they find themselves.

If children know themselves to be loved unconditionally, then they will feel more confident to strike out on their own to explore new environments and social groupings, and to reach out to someone else in need of their support. While this is not impossible for a child with low self-esteem to do, it is easier for someone who feels good about him or herself. Empathy might be withheld for other reasons, but confidence in one's self as an object of love by respected adults will not feature. Communications received by the child from the primary caregivers are extremely powerful and can work negatively against the ethos of a setting. Children quickly learn to adapt their behaviour to suit the situation. For example, racist name-calling, if prevalent in a home or the wider community, will often not be used in a pre-school setting where the children have learned that such language would not be tolerated by the staff. Practitioners can then be deceived into thinking that the children are unaware of the derogatory language being used in the community to demean those who are considered different. All the setting can do in such circumstances is to seek to provide the children with an alternative view and hope to engage in dialogue with the parents and carers, and members of the local community, to challenge their perceptions and to help them to face up to their fears. Children need safe places to talk about things that are puzzling or frightening them. If this is denied them, they will make their own kind of sense of a situation, which might be far from the truth and become damaging to them and to others in the future. Hopefully, their home will provide such a haven, but pre-school settings should certainly endeavour to create the kind of environment where it is possible to talk about difference and to celebrate the fact that we are all different. One way to enhance children's self-esteem is to allow them to use their knowledge and skills by sharing in the decision-making that directly affects them. It is vital that children with low self-esteem, or an over-inflated idea of their own superiority, be helped to see the true worth of every individual. Children in both situations, therefore, need to develop a healthy self-knowledge.

Self-knowledge

Children who are encouraged to think that they are superior to others are often told how wonderful they are and are praised for every offering, even if there has been minimal effort and the work falls far short of their best. These children soon recognise the fact that there is no need to strive to please. This is different from unconditional love; it is not helpful to the child. It deprives children of a genuine sense of achievement, and they may find it harder in later life to persevere with a challenging task. On the other hand, children who are persistently criticised or ridiculed can lose any motivation to keep on trying to achieve anything. Their response might be to withdraw into themselves or to lash out aggressively and to stop reflecting on their actions. Practitioners can help such children by giving them space to think and to be creative in a supportive environment, and by spending time listening to them and challenging them appropriately. As the children experience genuine interest in them as people and receive a realistic assessment of their achievements, they will begin to grow in confidence and to make judgements which are thoughtful and which enable them to gain a true sense of their own worth and that of others. They will also learn what is considered to be appropriate behaviour in a particular social context.

Social development

The stronger the bond a child has with a key adult, the more confident he or she will feel when moving out into the wider world and forming relationships with other people. The initial secure relationship then becomes the place of safety to retreat to for explanation, for reassurance and for rest. As time goes on, the time spent with others will increase as the child becomes more independent. As with parents and carers, the practitioners in the pre-school setting have an important responsibility to help the child to separate from the key adult and to build healthy relationships with peers and other adults. Very early on, children begin to respond to their peers and become interested in the reactions of those around them. Numerous messages are assimilated. Rohr and Ebert (2001) say that these are sometimes communicated verbally, for example, 'Always be nice and say thank you!' and sometimes non-verbally, for example, by displaying body language that says, 'Don't come too close to me!' Young children react to these messages by internalising certain ideals, for example, 'I am good if I keep quiet.' They begin to develop avoidance strategies to escape punishment or other unpleasant consequences and start to build up defence mechanisms. Children copy the behaviour they see around them and use these models as they develop their interactions with others, although the initial caregivers are still the focal point of their existence, the people to whom they turn to test out their understanding of the wider world. It is vital, therefore, for children's future well-being and role as responsible citizens that caregivers provide a helpful model and are able to be honest and admit, for example, when they have made a mistake. Also, they need to be willing to listen to the children and encourage them to talk about anything that puzzles or alarms them, especially as they become aware of sensations of guilt and shame when they feel they have not lived up to their own ideals, and they learn that others can be judgemental about their behaviour.

By the time children are three years old, their friendships have started to become important to them, although they are still short-lived. In terms of their relationships with adults, they will become aware that the key caregivers in their home and in their educational setting care for them in a similar way. They will support them through the day, helping them to manage their dressing, feeding, toileting and resting, while helping them to become increasingly independent. They will talk to them and try to get to know them better. They will show their concern for their progress and well-being. They will encourage their relationships with other children and with other adults by helping them to develop friendships. The years through to the end of the Foundation Stage should see children developing peer relationships and being able to sustain more than one relationship at a time, and to learn what it means to be a member of a group. This will include learning to empathise with others, to understand that others have different points of view and to learn with others. It will also mean coming to understand what friendship is about and how it works. At first, children will base their social behaviour on the family context, and, in the setting, they will still need a key adult to relate to, to help them to acquire the complex social skills needed to negotiate the relationships with other adults and children in this wider group. To understand these messages that the children are receiving, Robinson (2008) asks us to reflect on what feelings were encouraged or discouraged in our own family, and how these have affected the way we relate to other people. Do we, for example, try to avoid situations where we might get distressed? Do we avoid confrontations or get a bit embarrassed if someone gets too excited? Through observations of children's play, the practitioner will be able to monitor their social progress from playing alongside their peers to full cooperation and be able to discern the kinds of ideas they are assimilating from their intimate family group. If the scaffolding of their learning by adults and more experienced peers has been positive, they will gradually become more independent, be able to carefully think through the decisions they make. They will become capable of practising their friend-ship skills by reflecting on their own behaviour in relation to others and will, eventually, be able to take their place as a responsible member of society. How socially successful they become will depend very much on their emotional well-being.

Emotional development

Gardner (1993) held that both the aspects of knowing about one's own feelings and tuning in to the feelings of others involve emotions as a means of regulating behaviour. Robinson (2008) agrees, saying that our emotional health affects our levels of motivation, persistence and willingness to change, adapt and learn. In fact, it could be argued it is not just our *willingness,* but also our *ability* to change that is brought into question here. Goleman (1998: 24) speaks of our emotional competence as a learned capability based on our emotional intelligence that determines our potential for learn-ing the practical skills based on its five elements: self-awareness, motivation, self-regulation, empathy and adeptness in relationships. So how are very young children to develop their emotional intelligence? Gooch et al. (2003) say that very early language and involvement in imaginative play provide the opportunities children need to share and try out their feelings. In the first years of their life, children are experiencing everything for the first time, and the way they respond and make sense of what is happening to them and around them is through their emotions. They become aware of their own mood swings and begin to recognise the signs of other people's changing thoughts and feelings. These shifting emotions will first be observed in the home, and if families talk freely about their emotions then children are more likely to be able to share their feelings and to acquire the vocabulary to do so. Males are more likely to learn that it is improper for them to show their emotions, but sometimes the family ethos is such that the members of nei-ther gender express their love or care for each other, either physically or verbally. It is harder for children from such a home to begin to share their feelings, and they can suppress these, often to their detriment, or express them in inappropriate ways. We are all influenced by our early nurturing, and we learn from a very early age how to please the adults we depend on and adapt our behaviour accordingly. We tend to pick up the message from those around us that we need to avoid certain negative emotions and ensure that we can curb or control them when they arise in us. We therefore develop various defence mechanisms to help us cope. As they develop and experience a range of emotions, children become aware of what is expected of them by society in terms of their emotional expression. If they fail to live up to these ideals, they learn what it means to feel guilty. Practitioners need to help children to reflect on their behaviour because only then can they begin to take control of it. Carefully planned stories told with aids such as Persona Dolls (Brown 2001, 2008) and puppets can significantly help this reflection to take place, age appropriately, in a safe environment. The children explore a range of emotions and learn to empathise when someone is anxious or unhappy and can be helped to understand the more difficult concept of how someone can be both worried and cross at the same time. Through participating in such discussion sessions, the children can be encouraged to express their emotions, to empathise with others and to start to solve problems. This is vital for their emotional well-being because the more insight children gain into their own feelings, the more likely it is that they will be able to control their own behaviour. Long (2005: 10–14) talks of the *tags* that practitioners need in order to recognise what might be guiding the children's behaviour. For example, children may have been encouraged to 'be strong'. The strength of this encouragement for them might be that they become self-sufficient and require very little help. They work hard and help others. The downside might be that they find relationships difficult. They would like to be cared for and supported sometimes but find it difficult to ask for help, either practical or emotional, in case they are rejected. Long (2005: 10) says that such a child can then appear 'lonely, cold and aloof towards others'. The challenge for these children is to understand that making mistakes and asking for help is normal. Helping them to see that other children have similar weaknesses can increase their emotional insight and help them to share more of their feelings and not to be afraid that others will reject them. To get the best out of such children, Long advises giving praise and acknowledgement for their consideration, kindness and determination. Pushing them to share their feelings can be counterproductive, but modelling emotional literacy and giving them time on their own can be helpful.

Others *tags* include those who have assimilated the message that they need, above all to 'please others', 'be perfect', 'hurry up' or 'try hard'. Those struggling to live up to such ideals also need to be recognised by the practitioners and given careful attention. Strategies are needed to enable all children not only to discuss their feelings but also to curb their impulses by learning to delay their gratification. Turn-taking games, shared stories and circle-time activities based around the real concerns of the children can all contribute to helping them become emotionally competent. Children need to learn that it is important that we respect and acknowledge each other's feelings and opinions. Some emotions, such as anger, can be very frightening for children who have little experience of the world and do not realise that this is not a permanent state. They need help to understand how such strong emotions can be controlled and managed in future. As the DfES (2007b: 22) says, 'Children who are encouraged to feel free to express their ideas and their feelings, such as joy, sadness, frustration and fear, can develop strategies to cope with new, challenging or stressful situations.'

The adult perspective

Before we, as practitioners, begin to work with, and alongside, the children to support their personal, social and emotional development, it is vital that we take a long hard look at our own attitudes, strengths and weaknesses. From an adult perspective, we can sometimes view the things that worry children as trivial. It does us good from time to time to remember acts of discrimination that we have been involved in ourselves or have witnessed happening to others when we were growing up. Seemingly innocent name-calling can do much damage in a person's life and yet is brushed off so easily by the perpetrators, as 'Oh but, we were only children, we were just playing, we didn't mean any harm.'

We all have prejudices; it is inevitable because of the things that are said to us, and the messages we have assimilated as we were growing up. The important thing is to come to terms with this, to be brave enough to look at ourselves fairly and squarely. The shame is not in having acquired these prejudices, often unwittingly, but to deny they exist or having identified them not to actively seek to eradicate them. My mother being one of seven children, six girls and a boy, and my father one of four, three boys and a girl, I found myself as a child growing up in a very close-knit, loving extended family. However, one of my favourite aunts had an expression that I have found hard to shake off. She would often use the expression 'Dirty Arab'. I think it is extremely unlikely that she ever met anyone from Arabia, and had she done so would probably have discovered that they were Muslim and washed at least five times a day before their prayers, and hence were a lot cleaner than most of the British population (especially in those days before the wholesale institution of showers in the United Kingdom!).

However, it meant that, when my children were growing up, and my son came in caked in mud from an exhilarating game of football in the park opposite, it was often on the tip of my tongue to say, 'Ooh, you dirty Arab!' On reflection, here I was stereotyping a whole nation as being *dirty,* for no other reason than that I had heard my aunt say it so often; it came to my mind unbidden. If you think you have no prejudices, consider the parents and carers who walk through your door every day. Why is it that you get on with some people immediately, while you have to work really hard at the relationship with others? We excuse ourselves by saying there is a personality clash or the other party is just being awkward, but if we dig deep, we are likely to find a negative attitude that was born out of a past experience; equally, you may have no conscious idea of where it has come from. Lewis (2002: 128) said that if you think you are not conceited, it means you are very conceited indeed. I think the same could be said about prejudice. How easy it is, when we meet a caregiver for the first time, to categorise them according to their looks, their dress, their accent and the way they speak to their children? A practitioner once described how upset he became with a mother who always seemed to be criticising her child and demeaning her. His feelings were justified, but he was surprised by the virulence of his anger, to the extent of wanting to hit her, until he realised that this was what his own mother had done to him. Although some of us have a healthier start than others, we are all vulnerable, and we all need to maintain our vigilance in this area. As a staff, we need to create the kind of environment where we can express our feelings to each other and be critical friends. This is difficult, and none of us likes to think we are acting unjustly, are speaking without thought, or that while our words are wholly appropriate, our body language is screaming a denial of what we are saying. But, if we want to show the children a good model of how failures and mistakes can be confessed, disagreements put right, and differences can not only be tolerated but celebrated, then we have no option but to begin with ourselves.

What are Persona Dolls?

Persona Dolls are different from other dolls because they belong to the adults in a setting. They are used to try and prevent young children learning prejudiced attitudes and discriminatory behaviour while helping them unlearn any negative messages they might have already assimilated (Brown 1998). The dolls are given personalities, family and cultural backgrounds, likes and dislikes, and the stories that are created around them enable children to explore positive and negative emotions. In the process, children deepen their identification and friendship with the dolls, who become 'people' in the setting. The aim is to develop the children's ability to empathise with the dolls and to care about them, to recognise the ways in which they are similar to and different from them and to learn that discriminatory behaviour hurts. Through their identification with the dolls, children are helped to see the injustice of the situations being presented to them in the stories and are motivated to think of solutions. Being put in the role of problem-solver and decision-maker, and having their ideas treated with respect, helps boost the children's self-esteem and confidence. Having heard stories in which the dolls are unfairly treated, they are more likely to react positively when someone is excluded from play, teased or bullied. Incidents that have already happened in the setting can be paralleled by a story from the doll told in such a way that neither the perpetrator nor the victim feels that they are being targeted. Persona Dolls are highly valued across the world for the contribution they make to the personal, social and emotional development of children. (For training information, see www.persona-doll-training.org.)

Why story?

When Vivien Gussin Paley was nearing the end of her career in early child education, she decided that she had had enough of the careless way in which some children excluded others from their play. This constant rejection was having a devastating effect on those children who, when they asked if they could play, were mostly told, 'No', and the sound of that rejection resounded 'like a slap from wall to wall' (Paley 1993: 3). Paley decided to raise the issue in her kindergarten by introducing a new regime. The rule would be that 'You can't say you can't play.' With her pupils and with the older children whom she drew into the debate, her idea was met with scepticism, if not downright hostility. Paley records that only four children out of the twenty-five in the kindergarten were in favour, and these were the children most often rejected. The idea was not to end all friendship choices but to force the children to take responsibility for involving anyone who asked to join in their game, rather than what usually happened, that a practitioner would foist a neglected child onto a group, which only caused resentment. In spite of the less than enthusiastic response, Paley announced the new regime, but wrote:

Fortunately, the human species does not live by debate alone. There is an alternative route, proceeding less directly, but often better able to reach the soul of a controversy. It is *story*, the children's preferred frame of reference. This time, however, *I* will be the storyteller, inventing Magpie, a bird who rescues those who are lonely and frightened and tells them stories to raise their spirits.

(Paley 1993: 4)

Stories are so powerful because every individual is living his or her own story. When we come together to share our experiences, we are sharing our stories, and, through these stories, we influence each other's lives. The crucial element is always the relevance of the content. Whether the story is a true life tale or one created by the storyteller, there must be points of connection, and the stronger these are, the more the listeners will engage. Belief is suspended at any age, if the issues are pertinent. The context may be one that carries the listener into realms of fantasy, but if the characters display a range of emotions that we recognise and have to make decisions in the same way as we do, then we can identify with them in that story. Story can take us into situations outside of our experience and help us to learn from someone else's endeavours, another's pain and pleasure, to empathise and to solve problems on behalf of others and, in so doing, change our own perspective on life. Three-year-old children begin to make judgements based on the messages they have received from the adults around them in the home, in the street and on the television, and their behaviour is influenced by these models. So, even at this tender age, stories must be ready to challenge discriminatory thoughts and actions that are already beginning to take root. Children need to feel good about themselves, but not because they are superior to someone else or because society has decreed that it is better to be white than black, or it is better to be a girl than a boy. Story is a universal mode of transferring ideas and exploring emotions, crossing cultural and religious boundaries and bridging age, gender and ability differences. In the sections below, story is used to scaffold children's reflection on themselves as people in their own social context with a view to strengthening their emotional well-being and helping them to become responsible citizens, able to conform for the common good but confident to stand alone, if necessary, to challenge greed, cruelty and injustice and to become truly free. This is not freedom in the sense of licence to do as they please, and thus limiting the freedom of others, but the freedom to be compassionate, generous risk-takers who are able to say no to their own indulgences and to be imaginative in finding solutions to the problems that divide friends and neighbours, both those next door and those on the other side of the world.

References

Brown, B. (1998) *Unlearning Discrimination in the Early Years,* Stoke-on-Trent: Trentham Books.

—— (2001) *Combating Discrimination: Persona Dolls in Action,* Stoke-on-Trent: Trentham Books. (See also www.persona-doll-training.org.)

—— (2008) *Equality in Action: A Way Forward with Persona Dolls,* Stoke-on-Trent: Trentham Books.

DfES (2007a) *Statutory Framework for the Early Years Foundation Stage: Every Child Matters: Change for Children,* Nottingham: DfES publications.

—— (2007b) *Practice Guidance for the Early Years Foundation Stage: Every Child Matters: Change for Children,* Nottingham: DfES publications.

Dowling, M. (2005) *Young Children's Personal, Social and Emotional Development,* 2nd edn, London: Paul Chapman.

Ekman, P. (2003) *Emotions Revealed: Recognizing Faces and Feelings to Improve Communication,* New York: Times Books.

Gardner, H. (1993) *Multiple Intelligences,* New York: Basic Books.

Goleman, D. (1998) *Working with Emotional Intelligence,* London: Bloomsbury.

Gooch, D. T., Powell, K. and Abbott, L. (2003) *Birth to Three Matters: A Review of the Literature,* London: DfES Publishing.

Lewis, C. S. (2002) *Mere Christianity,* London: HarperCollins.

Long, R. (2005) *Children's Thoughts and Feelings,* London: David Fulton.

Paley, V. G. (1993) *You Can't Say You Can't Play,* Cambridge, Mass.: Harvard University Press.

Robinson, M. (2008) 'Child Development: Your Guide to the First Five Years: Part 3 Emotional Development', *Nursery World,* January. Available online at www.nurseryworld.co.uk/news/login/815763 (accessed 2 July 2008).

Rohr, R. and Ebert, A. (2001) *The Enneagram: A Christian Perspective,* New York: The Crossroad Publishing Company.

Dispositions and attitudes

From birth–20 months

Development matters

- Develop an understanding and awareness of themselves.

- Learn that they have influence on and are influenced by others.

- Learn that experiences can be shared.

- Become aware of themselves as separate from others.

- Discover more about what they like and dislike.

- Have a strong exploratory impulse.

- Explore the environment with interest.

Key words

self-awareness, exploration

Main story: *Baby's Busy World*
(D. Sirett (2005), Dorling Kindersley Publishing, London)

This book opens up the opportunity to explore with the children a developing awareness of their own bodies and their immediate environment.

Aspects of a child's body are named and faces displayed that show a variety of feelings: happy, sad, grumpy, shy, cheeky, tired, sleepy, thirsty. Food and clothes are another centre of attention, as are games, bath time, vehicles, animals and baby 'helping out'.

Activities

- Talk, or sing or make rhymes up about all the items involved in the routine activities of feeding, changing nappies, bathing, preparing for sleep. For example, a lullaby can be a traditional song but need not be; a gentle rocking rhythm of half-humming and half-reciting what you see and hear will do just as well. In our house, the bedtime rhyme: 'Diddle diddle dumpling my son John went to bed with his trousers on', became 'Diddle, diddle dumpling, my son Justin went to bed in a galvanised dustbin' (perhaps not much of an inducement to sleep!).

- During nappy changing, or before and after bathing, leave some time for the baby to kick without a nappy. Free movement of arms and legs will allow babies to explore their own bodies and find out what they can do. These early stretching and waving movements will soon lead to rolling and crawling.

- Make bubbles with some washing-up liquid and blow them within the baby's visual field and then, as they develop, blow them within their reach. At first, they will simply follow the bubbles, but later they will begin to discover what they can do and will find ways of letting you know what they really enjoy.

- Give the baby plenty of focused one-to-one time, respond to their movements, gently tap their cheeks and tickle them, while continuing to talk to them. Encourage any sounds or smiles with an immediate response; this is the earliest form of 'conversation', of turn-taking.

- Massaging babies is very common in many parts of the world and is increasing in popularity in the United Kingdom. Many claim that this kind of gentle stroking of any part of the baby's body has health benefits, but here we are concerned particularly with the fact that it can help babies to become aware of their own body.

Make sure your hands are warm and you are in a warm room; use a little oil if you prefer (olive oil is fine). Scented oils can be problematic, as the baby is bound to ingest some at some point by sucking their hands or their toes! Opinion is divided about whether newborn babies should be massaged, but some insist that it is beneficial for premature babies. Certainly, desist if the baby is ill, or is obviously not enjoying the experience. Permission will have to be given from parents and carers for this activity to be carried out because of child-protection issues.

- As the babies grow, they can be encouraged to point to their head, their nose, their mouth, their eyes and their ears and begin to join in simple songs such as 'Heads, shoulders, knees and toes' and 'Wind the bobbin up'.

- Mirrors can help children to become aware of themselves as individuals. Babies will begin to focus on their own image when they are held close to a large mirror and will be interested by the face they see, although at first they will not recognise it as their own. Gradually, they will begin to explore different kinds of mirrors and notice how their reflection changes and enjoy dancing around in front of a mirror in a safe environment. We all need to establish a sense of self; otherwise, it is not possible for us to remember events that happen to us.

- Tie books with appropriate fastenings to the side of the baby's cot or pram for them to touch and explore at any time. Choose board books, or those made out of cloth or plastic, that use strongly contrasting colours. Exploring such books with small babies will help their attachment to their key carer and will help them develop an awareness of themselves, discovering what they like and what they do not.

Look, listen and note

- During all kinds of water play, whether bathing or with bubbles in a bowl, the practitioner should note the baby's preferences and how these are being expressed.

- Note the baby's response to the establishment of daily routines. Their very earliest reactions will be to light and to warmth and to being held close where they can feel the heartbeat of the adult cradling them, but very soon the voices of key adults and other children will become associated with these events, and they will begin to make sense of their environment and their place within it as an individual.

- Look out for the ways in which the baby is communicating their likes and dislikes. Contented gurgling and screaming will become refined and as choices of, for example, fruits and vegetables are offered, an open mouth for more or spitting out will eventually be replaced by violent nods or head-shaking gradually accompanied as the power of speech develops, by 'No', with a turning away of the head and tight lips, or an eager 'Yes', accompanied by a nodding head.

- When looking at a book, observe the baby's reactions to the different words and pictures expressed by their body movements and any contented or excited sounds.

- When 'making music', note how the baby responds to show their likes and dislikes of different sounds. They may gurgle, babble, laugh or scream! They may show a preference through body movements and expressions or by choosing particular 'instruments'.

- Observe the baby's reaction to their own image in a mirror. Note at what stage they begin to realise that it is their own reflection.

Effective practice

- When you are making up rhymes and songs to accompany various routines, make sure you show the baby items as you name them or, if you are referring, for example, to their toes or fingers or cheeks, then gently stroke that part of their body. As the baby develops, you can begin to point to your own features and then to the baby's as they become more aware of their own body as a separate entity.

- Give the baby a choice wherever possible and follow up their interests, building on the responses they make and trying to keep the 'conversation' going. This will necessitate the provision of a variety and range of items to excite their curiosity, different music to become attuned to and plenty of books to share.

Planning and resourcing

- You are the baby's most important resource in the setting. Your time and attention are vital to their well-being and development, and your one-to-one sessions need to be planned for and protected.

- Provide items for the baby to make their own music as well as providing CDs of a variety of soothing instrumental music as well as rhymes and songs.

- Keep a range of cot, bath and board books for children to access themselves and for you to share together.

Home links

- Initially find out from the parents and carers any preferences the baby may have for particular activities and share the baby's likes and dislikes that you have discovered.

- Parents and carers will be doing many of these activities at home in tandem with what is going on in the setting. Especially share the importance of 'cot' books and put them in touch with a group such as Bookstart if they are unaware of it.

- Communication on progress must be shared, and where this is difficult because there is no common language, then an interpreter must be found. Gestures and miming can help in a limited way, but important information must be understood and the opportunity provided for worries to be shared.

Additional stories

Birkett, G. (2008) (illustrator) *Is This My Nose?* London: Red Fox Publications. (Five different children are asked by animals if they can find various features. It ends with a mirror for the baby to look in. A multicultural board book with very simple, appealing illustrations.)

Inkpen, M. (2006) *Wibbly Pig Likes Bananas,* London: Hodder Children's Books. (This board book explores Wibbly Pig's likes, from bananas to hats, and asks the children for their preferences.)

Kubler, A. (2003) *Heads, Shoulders, Knees and Toes,* London: Mantra Lingua. (An interactive board book based on the familiar song of the same name, available in English and in more than ten bilingual editions.)

MacKinnon, D. (1996) *All about Me,* London: Frances Lincoln. (An activity-based book of beautiful photographs designed to help young children learn about the different parts of their bodies.)

—— (2002) *Babies' Favourites,* London: Frances Lincoln. (Eight sets of objects are hidden under flaps for the children to find and to decide on their own preferences. The sets include clothes, food, pets and toys.)

—— (2003) *Baby's First Year,* London: Frances Lincoln. (A series of 'firsts' as a baby boy is followed through his first year. Engaging photographs are combined with a delightful text.)

Niland, D. (2006) *When I Was a Baby,* London: Puffin Books. (A 'big' boy thinks about how he liked to snuggle in his blanket when he was a little baby. Now he has given his blanket to his new baby sister.)

Stockham, J. (2006) *Looking Good! Just Like Me!* Swindon: Child's Play. (Board book. Babies will love lifting the flaps to find out all about themselves including their feelings, features, abilities, tastes.)

From 16–36 months

Development matters

- Learn that they are special through the responses of adults to individual differences and similarities.

- Develop a curiosity about things and processes.

- Take pleasure in learning new skills.

- Show their particular characteristics, preferences and interests.

- Begin to develop self-confidence and a belief in themselves.

Key words

self-belief, curiosity

Main story: *What I Like*
(C. Anholt and L. Anholt (2006), Walker Books, London)

In this book, six children talk about their likes and dislikes, which include references to ice cream, a funny dream, a place to hide, a pony ride and bumps, lumps and dumps. It touches on their experiences at nursery school, the friendships they make and what it means to grow up. It combines a simple rhyming text with full colour illustrations and is useful to stimulate talk around the children's own sense of themselves and their developing relationships with those around them and their environment. It can be used in conjunction with the Anholts' two other books on the same theme (see in the list below for details). *I Like Me* includes the wonderfully affirming statement, 'When I like me, I can do anything at all.' Similarly, *I Like Me, I Like You* addresses the need children have to feel good about themselves: their bodies, their feelings and their achievements, but also the need to learn to be tolerant of others.

Activities

- Continue to encourage the children's increasing awareness of them-selves and their own abilities. Show appreciation of actions under-taken by the children to show their knowledge of a new skill. This can be their first intelligible words or their first steps. Equally, it can be a process they have observed and in which they now want to participate, for example: taking the clothes out of the washing machine and placing them in the clothes basket or tumble drier, fetching their shoes when it is time to go outside, putting their soiled nappy bag in the appropriate place. I was intrigued to observe my grandson carrying out this latter activity. When he first picked up the bag, my daughter wondered where he was going with it, but he placed it carefully by the french windows. She realised then that he had observed her putting the bags outside, and this was the nearest he could get to that collection point. When adults respond to any such action by clapping and saying 'clever boy' or 'clever girl', this will often be repeated by the child. Sometimes a response is drawn from adults because they find an action amus-ing, and the child is quick to spot this and to repeat the action. For example, children who say, 'Uh-oh!' every time they drop some-thing often bring a smile from those around, and the phrase is thus reinforced. Photographs of the child can be taken following such a process in the setting. For example:

    - Picture 1: Items ready for a nappy change: the mat, the wipes, some talcum powder, a bag for the used nappy, a fresh nappy.

    - Picture 2: The child on the changing mat having a clean nappy put on.

    - Picture 3: The child putting the used nappy in a sealed bag in the nappy bin (or at a suitable collection point where it can be dealt with by an adult).

    Such pictures of simple processes like this can be made into a poster to be placed at child height around the room in appropriate areas.

- Finger and toe rhymes are useful in increasing children's bodily awareness and also their social development, for example: 'This little piggy went to market', 'Round and round the garden like a teddy bear', 'Tommy thumb, Tommy thumb where are you?' and 'Two little dickie birds sitting on the wall, one called Peter, one called Paul'. Such traditional rhymes can be performed either with one key adult or adapted to suit particular groups. Right from the beginning, it is important to have ethnic, cultural and religious differences of your children in mind. For example, religious practices for those of a Jewish or Muslim faith exclude the consumption of pig meat in any form. This often leads to pigs being regarded as unclean animals, so, for some families, songs and stories about pigs would not be appropriate. Similarly, dogs wander the streets in many countries and are regarded as vermin that carry disease in the same way as rats might be thought of in Britain. However, the rhyme could easily be changed to, 'This little chicken went to market' and cried, 'Cheep, cheep, cheep all the way home.' Likewise, the story of the three little pigs could be changed to three little goats. However, it is always better to ask families how they feel and not to make assumptions. Some families will have no objections at all but will still be pleased that you were thoughtful enough to ask what their feelings are. Rhymes such as 'Two little dickie birds', can be used to boost a child's sense of self by replacing the names of the birds with the names of children in the group. For example, 'one called Shahnaz, one called Sam'.

- Support decisions that the child makes: 'Look, Leroy has put pink icing on his cake'; 'Emily has chosen green tissue for her card'. If children see that small decisions like this are noticed by practitioners, then they will feel valued and encouraged to be more adventurous. At the end of sessions, the children can show the product of their activity, and rhymes can be made. For example, to the rhythm of 'Peter hammers with one hammer', you can use the words, 'Leroy cooks with pink icing, pink icing, pink icing, Leroy cooks with pink icing on his cake.' Or, 'Emily glues with green tissue, green tissue, green tissue. Emily glues with green tissue on her card.' Using the children's names in this way helps to keep their interest at the end of a session when they will be feeling tired, and it will boost their sense of achievement and give them renewed confidence for their next activity, whether this is in the setting or at home.

- Provide sturdy board books that the children can read or play with whenever they wish; ones that they can hold themselves and turn the pages at will. This control over the page-turning will give them a sense of their own ability, and the content of the books will help develop their sense of identity. Being able to choose from a variety of books will help them to begin decision-making and to discover what their preferences are. Choosing a book for a particular purpose will enhance these affirmations (see home links below).

Look, listen and note

- Make a note when you see the children taking part in a routine activity that shows they observed a process carefully.

- Record whether they clap themselves after performing a certain action or show some form of approval.

- Observe the development of the children's decision-making skills. This may be a choice of activity or particular book to read to themselves or to bring for an adult to share. Practitioner observations of these early stages of independent reading will provide vital evidence for the children's profile and their progress in this area.

Effective practice

Make sure that the children are able to make a contribution to the group and that their offering is valued. This may mean using someone who shares their first language, or putting mechanisms into place to enable them to contribute non-verbally by gesturing or pointing to pictures. Attitudes to the expression of feelings differ across cultures and between families. In some countries, people of both sexes greet each other by kissing and hugging, while others would consider this most improper. Views of personal space differ between people, as do attitudes to achievement; for some, group achievement is applauded rather than individual achievement. All of this will mean paying particular attention to a child's family, linguistic, cultural and religious background.

Planning and resourcing

- A digital camera will need to be available to capture stages of regular routines in the setting. These can then be transferred to the computer, printed off and laminated for use as wall displays or mounted onto stiff cardboard to make your own books to add to the commercially produced board books that you always have available.

- Other items, such as a little olive oil for massage, can easily be provided from the kitchen, if permission has been granted for a gentle massage.

Home links

- Find out as much information as you can from parents and carers about their religious, cultural and ethnic background. To share such knowledge will make parents and carers feel welcome and valued and will enable practitioners to learn new ways of doing things which might be different but which are not 'wrong'. If language is a barrier, then an exchange of photographs can demonstrate every-day activities and special celebrations. Pictures of the child in different contexts will enable you to evaluate their confidence.

- Encourage parents to buy and borrow library books for the children and let them choose which ones to take, for example, on holiday, when visiting grandparents or when the family is undergoing an important change such as moving house. Stories can also help to prepare children for a new baby in the family or for the death of a grandparent.

Additional stories

Anholt, C. and Anholt, L. (2001) *I Like Me, I Like You,* London: Dorling Kindersley Publishers. (See above under main story.)

—— (2001) *I Like Me,* London: Dorling Kindersley. (See above under main story.)

—— (2006) *What Makes Me Happy?* London: Walker Books. (A chance to explore what makes you laugh and cry, what makes you bored, excited or scared but, most of all, what makes you happy.)

Benjamin, A. H. (1999) *A Duck So Small,* London: Little Tiger Press. (Duffle Duck is much smaller than the other ducks, and everything he tries to do goes wrong. The others tease him and say, 'A duck so small can do nothing at all.' Duffle starts to believe them until one day his small size is just what's needed.)

Gray, K. (2005) *Yuk!* London: Red Fox. (Daisy has been asked to be a bridesmaid for her Auntie Sue but wants to wear her football kit, or scuba gear, or her leopard-skin suit, but in the end she compromises and is allowed to design her own dress.)

Hutchins, P. (2001) *Titch,* London: Tandem Library. (Titch is the youngest of three, and his big brother and sister have bigger bikes, their kites fly higher and their instruments make more noise, but when he sows a tiny seed, they are all amazed at how high it grows.)

Simpson-Enock, S. (2008) *Mummy, Mummy, What's in Your Tummy?* London: Frances Lincoln. (A lift-the-flap book for a child whose mother is expecting a new baby but who is unsure as yet why it is that her tummy is getting bigger and bigger. The child in this story imagines all sorts of things being inside: a fairy with wings? A boat painted blue? The Man in the Moon?)

From 30–60+ months

Development matters

- Seek and delight in new experiences.

- Have a positive approach to activities and events.

- Show confidence in linking up with others for support and guidance.

- Show increasing independence in selecting and carrying out activities.

- Display high levels of involvement in activities.

- Persist for extended periods of time at an activity of their choosing.

Early learning goals

- Continue to be interested, excited and motivated to learn.

- Be confident to try new activities, initiate ideas and speak in a familiar group.

- Maintain attention, concentrate, and sit quietly when appropriate.

Key words

self-confidence, new experiences, persistence

Main story: *The Monkey and the Panda*
(A. Barber (1996), Frances Lincoln, London)

In the story, the Monkey is described as being lean, lithe and lively, while the Panda is fat, furry and friendly. The children of the village appreciate the attributes of both these creatures, depending on whether they want to play noisily or to rest somewhere comfortable. However, the Monkey becomes jealous of the Panda, thinking that the children love him the most, and he starts to act very wildly to try and keep their attention. The villagers are a kindly people and do not wish to hurt the Monkey but they soon become tired of his behaviour and want to get rid of him. In the end, they decide to ask the advice of the wise old monk who lives nearby.

This story will be useful to begin some discussion about how we are all different and to celebrate that fact. Begin by asking the children about why the village children loved the Monkey and the Panda, and why they needed them both. Questions can be extended along the lines of:

- Why did the Monkey think that the children loved the Panda the most?
- Why did his actions upset people?
- Was he right to feel jealous?
- Do you feel jealous sometimes?
- How does that make you feel?
- What did the villagers do to solve the problem?
- Can we learn anything from this story?
- What did you like best about the story? Why?
- What part didn't like you like? Why?

For circle time, help everyone to affirm themselves by saying who they are and what they are good at. For example, 'I am Gurjit. I can do up my coat.' Then move on to what they like doing, or what they find difficult, or are afraid of. For example, 'I am Holly. I like listening to stories.' 'I am Ayinda. I can't run fast.' Or, 'I am Harry. I don't like loud bangs.'

We have a responsibility to help the children to understand that we all have things we are good at and things we find difficult and things that scare us, but together we can learn to help each other, and we can be proud of the things we do well, without becoming jealous of what someone else can do, or what they have, or what they look like. That will only make us feel sad or lead us to act in a mean way. We all have our preferences, things that we choose to do first and things we do not like doing. Sometimes our friends like to do the same things as us, and sometimes not; that is what makes us unique, makes us interesting and helpful to the people around us, and helps us to learn new skills and further develop our own talents.

Activities

- These games confirm the fact that we are all different, unique people, but that we can share similarities with others, for example our preferences and our dislikes, our excitements and our fears, and that this is a cause for celebration. Be sensitive to each child's reaction to talking about his or her feelings or being in a new situation: always have the option to pass in a game.

- The children sit in a circle on chairs, facing inwards. An adult stands in the centre and calls out a child's name. That child then gets up and says their name, for example: 'I am Mai.' The adult then sits in that child's place, and the child in the middle calls out some-one else's name, and the process is repeated. Alternatively, all the children can begin by standing in a ring without chairs, and, as their name is called by the practitioner, they say their name (for example, 'I am Amir') and sit down on the floor. Sometimes another child can call out the names, or the child who has just sat down calls out the new name.

- The children sit with an adult in a circle on chairs, facing inwards. One child is asked, 'What is your favourite game?' The child gives an answer, and then any others who share his or her interest change chairs. For this activity, there are enough chairs, so no one is 'out'. Other children then take turns to share their favourite game. On another day, the children can share one of the following they like best: food, clothes, pet, TV programme, game, toy, story, song or colour.

- Alternatively, with one chair too few, someone is always in the middle and that person can choose the criterion, for example: 'If you like fish fingers, change chairs', or 'If you have a dog, change chairs.' If you like, you can have a signal for the change, and the child in the middle can blow a whistle, ring a bell or shake a tambourine. You can also bring in items that you don't like as well as those you do, for example: 'If you don't like spiders, change chairs', and you can extend this to things you are good at and things that scare you.

Bodily awareness

Create activities that help the children to become aware of their own bodies and to appreciate their individuality.

- Sitting in a circle, set off a chain reaction. At first, the adult in the group will begin the action, but once the children get the idea, they can take the initiative. The action needs to involve some part of the body and should be accompanied by the words, where possible, but accept the action alone where children are going through a silent period prior to expressing themselves in English, have speech and language difficulties, or where there is any other reason that would otherwise prevent them from participating in the game. The actions could include: nod your head, shake your head, close your eyes, touch your nose, shake your hands, clap your hands, wiggle your fingers, pat your knees, stamp your feet, touch your toes, waggle your tongue. Later on, if the children can cope, try two actions together, for example, nod your head *and* stamp your feet. Encourage the children to wait until the person next to them turns to them and performs the action.

- Sometimes the actions can be performed in unison as part of a story or a rhyme, for example, wiggling fingers from high to low to simulate rain falling, or joining in finger rhymes (as above).

- Play musical statues or musical bumps. The children dance on the floor, and, when the music stops, they freeze or sit down, as appropriate. Praise those who sit down first or who hold their position for the longest without moving. Allow everyone to continue with no one being 'out'.

- Create a magic wand that changes the children into another shape. This can be a follow-up to a story involving different animals and birds or to a process such as a seed growing into a beautiful flower or tree. Talk about the characteristics of each new shape. This will involve the children thinking about their own bodies and how they can use them to simulate different shapes. They will become aware of what is possible and where their imagination needs to take over. Some roles will require the children to be noisy and others will require them to be quiet. Take some time afterwards to talk about being noisy and quiet. Invite the children to say which they prefer to be: 'I like to be noisy/quiet because ...' This would tie in well with the story of the Monkey and the Panda.

- Identify different activities and encourage the children to point to the correct part of their body. For example:

  - thinking   →   point to the head;
  - running   →   point to the legs and feet;
  - breathing →   point to the chest;
  - waving   →   point to the arms and hands.

  Attach actions to the different activities. This will help the children to connect the action with the correct vocabulary and will be especially helpful for children learning English as an additional language.

- Encourage the children to look at their image in a full-length mirror and to point to their various body parts.

Senses

- Focusing on the senses:

  - point to ears for hearing;
  - point to the eyes for looking;
  - point to the hands for touching;
  - point to the mouth for tasting;
  - point to the nose for smelling.

  The story *Welcome to the World Baby* or *My Body: A First Board Book* would also be useful here, see pp. 173 and 153 for details.

- As a follow-up to reading a book like *All Kinds of Bodies,* get the children in a small group and, with the adult, to place their hands in the middle of the circle and to compare them: the skin tone, the length and width of the fingers, the length of the fingernails. Ask the children what they notice. Other parts of the body can then receive similar attention.

- As a follow-up to reading a book like *Hair*, compare the hair differences in a small group:

  - whether someone's hair is curly (tight curls/loose curls) or wavy or straight;
  - what colour it is;
  - whether it is long or short;
  - what it feels like.

  The establishment of a hairdressing salon will be a useful follow-up to this activity and will provide opportunities for a number of skills to be developed: tending hair, making and recording appointments, collecting payments and providing a cup of tea for the customers.

Taste

- Take four different fruits and cut them up with the children. Let each child taste the different fruits and say which one they liked the best. Make a graph of their favourites. Try to include at least one fruit that would be familiar to all the children. Increase the range, or try different fruits on another occasion. If you have children from different ethnic backgrounds, then take the opportunity to talk about the fruits they enjoy at home and include some of these. Give the children small amounts of fruits they have not tried before, in case they have an allergic reaction.

- Explore the four main tastes: bitter, sweet, sour and salty. You could use slices of lemon, sweetened orange juice, salted crisps and plain chocolate. Give the children hand-held unbreakable mirrors to look at their tongues. Talk about the tongue and how it helps us to taste our food. Make a graph of the children's likes and dislikes. Encourage them to use the correct vocabulary but also list the words the children use to describe the tastes. Build in an element of prediction before the sampling exercise. Afterwards, they can talk about whether they were right, or not.

Smell

To introduce the smelling exercise, ask the children to close their eyes and spray a little perfume into the air. What can you smell? Talk about our noses and look at them in the mirror. Film canisters are useful for this activity. A pinprick hole in the lid will still allow any smell to be detectable. It is sometimes helpful to soak a cotton-wool ball with any liquid substances. The following provide distinctive smells for the children to identify: onions, vinegar, perfume, banana chunk, coffee granules, lemon oil, peppermint essence, cinnamon, marmite and cloves. Select a few from these or put together your own list. The children may not be able to name all the substances, but they will be able to describe the smell and say whether it is pleasant or not, or whether it reminds them of a place or a person.

Sight

- Look in a hand-held mirror and talk about your reflection. You might want to describe it as being like a picture of your face. Invite the children to do the same with their own unbreakable mirrors. Talk about where else they might be able to see their faces reflected. Afterwards, go for a walk both inside and outside of the setting, looking for places where the children can see their reflection. They will discover that they can see themselves in other mirrors, windows, water, tin foil, metal spoons (noting the difference, when looking at the concave or the convex side, of the upside-down image) and other metal appliances. In small groups, encourage the children to explore their own faces more closely with their small mirrors. Let them bring the mirrors up really close to their eyes, noses and mouths and then hold the mirrors at a distance to notice the effects. Show them how to breathe on the glass and then let it clear. Talk about what happens and why.

- Leave the mirrors for the children in an accessible place with other items found on your walk, such as metal spoons, a clear plastic bowl of water, some tin foil for the children to use on their own. Also provide drawing materials and crayons nearby for the children to draw pictures of themselves. Have colouring materials available in many different skin tones, so the children can choose the one resembling their own skin tone.

- Play 'What's missing?' with a small group of children. Put out some items on a tray. One child turns his or her back while another child removes one item. The first child turns back and tries to identify what is missing. The number of items can be as small or large as the children can cope with, while still being challenged. All the items could be different, such as a car, a brick and a spade, or they could be the same but distinguished by colour or shape, for example a red, blue, yellow and green ball, or four different yellow shapes: a circle, a square, a triangle, an oblong. This game will help to stimulate the children's visual memory and social skills as they learn to take their turn. A child with visual impairment can participate in this game by feeling the objects instead of viewing them.

Hearing

- In preparation for some listening games, go on a sound walk indoors and outdoors. Ask the children what sounds they think they might hear and record these on a large sheet of paper. Stop at regular intervals and get the children to listen with their eyes closed. Then share the sounds and record them for later discussions and for displays. Other sounds may be heard while the children are walking, such as their shoes on the gravel or a lorry driving past, and these can be included too. On return to the setting, check the children's predictions. How many of the sounds did you actually hear? Were there some unexpected sounds? These exercises all serve to help the children distinguish between different sounds and to listen actively.

- Give one of the children a bell, a small drum or pipe and ask him or her to hide. The child then uses the instrument to make a sound to attract the others who try to find them by following the sound. The instrument can be blown, shaken or beaten intermittently, or continuously. The children who are hiding will enjoy experimenting. They may want to begin quietly and increase the sound if the others are having difficulty finding them or, alternatively, begin loud and produce a softer sound as the others come nearer to their hiding place.

- Read a story to the children followed by some discussion of the storyline and the characters. Then read the story again, but this time ask the children to listen for a certain word – perhaps the name of one of the main characters – and, every time that name appears, to mark it in some way, for example, by putting their hands on their head or patting their knee. Children who rely on signing can also respond when they see the name being signed by the storyteller.

- Tape one of the children's voices saying a rhyme, and later play it back to the others and see if they can say whose voice it is. This will help the children to understand more about the similarities and differences that we have. Most of us have a voice to speak, but we all sound slightly different. This game can be extended by the children listening to each other on an intercom system, or the tape could be made available in the listening corner for them to play to themselves using headphones.

- Copy the sound: the adult begins by making a sound associated with a feeling, for example, crying. The children then copy the sound and pretend to cry. Ask the children, 'If we are crying, what do we feel like?' A laugh can be used as a happy sound, 'Grrr' for an angry sound and a gasp for an excited sound. Once the sounds have been established, then the children can take turns to begin the game.

- To help the children experience silence, pass musical instruments round very carefully so that they do not make a sound. Begin with one, and then add a second and a third, as the children's fine motor skills develop. If a sound does emanate from an instrument, it will be heard more acutely as it breaks into the silence.

- Form a circle with one child blindfolded in the centre. Place some keys on the floor for the child to 'guard'. The others try to take them in turn. The child in the centre points when he or she hears a noise. If the child points directly at the one who was making the sound, then they change places.

- Pass on a clapping rhythm. This can go round the circle. When it comes back to the adult, he or she can change the pattern, or name a child who can set off a new rhythm. Children with hearing impairment can join in by viewing the pattern, or by holding a drum on which they can feel the vibrations of a rhythm.

Touch

Any games that involve touch as the sensual focus are particularly helpful for pupils with visual impairment, who can join in with everyone else and can participate fully.

- A collection of items is placed in a big bag with a drawstring so that the children cannot look inside. These items may be viewed beforehand by the children. They then take turns to come and put their hand (or two hands) into the bag. They grasp one item and guess what it is before pulling it out. The practitioner can help by asking questions such as:

  - Is it hard or soft?
  - Is it round?
  - Is it fluffy?

  The children then pull out the objects to see if their guesses were correct. Alternatively, the children can describe the object to each other, and they can guess what the object is. This can be played with toys, musical instruments, different fruits or vegetables as well as with classroom objects. If the children do not know the name of the object for developmental reasons or because they are learning English as an additional language, have picture cards available or a duplicate of the objects in view, for the children to point to. The name of an object given in the child's first language should be accepted and indeed encouraged alongside the English word.

- Collect a variety of textured materials for the children to feel and talk about. Help the children to sort into sets the things that feel the same or similar by asking them questions about the attributes of the materials. These should include natural materials such as pieces of tree bark and leaves as well as manufactured materials, such as tinfoil, sandpaper and plastic items, and textiles, such as cotton, linen, wool and silk. Give the children the option of choosing a particular pile of material to glue onto a sheet of card to make a collage. They can work collaboratively on any of the sheets. When these are finished, and are dry, they can be stapled together to make a book. The children can describe the page they have made, and you should note the words and phrases they use. Place the book on display for the children to feel at any time with their descriptive words and phrases recorded on the facing page or on a separate sheet near to the display.

- Painting with fingers, hands and feet needs adult supervision but is a tactile experience that gives the children an added awareness of their own bodies and their own unique 'print'. The process of having your feet washed by someone else, which is likely to happen with very small children, can be a nurturing experience.

Meditation

Simple meditative-type activities can be experienced for short periods with very young children. They can listen to sounds around them, or to music, or focus on a particular object such as a candle or a singing bowl – a bowl that makes a ringing sound when it is tapped with a stick or when someone traces around the rim with a finger. Initially, yoga exercises should be introduced to the setting by a professional, but they can be highly beneficial for children from the age of three (see www. inspiredkids.co.uk, or contact your local health or leisure centre). Classes for three- to five-year-olds aim to be fun but also seek to stimulate the imagination. The relaxation techniques are often introduced through storytelling. At this early stage, yoga exercises:

- encourage body awareness and, through the physical activity, the children keep flexible as well as grow in strength and develop their coordination skills;

- are conducted in an enabling environment in which there is no competitive element; rather, cooperation and compassion are engendered between the children;

- help the children to feel calm and to relax.

Look, listen and note

- Observe the children's reactions to their peers and to other adults. Note where children appear confident and where they appear anxious, where they are absorbed totally in an activity and where their interest is short-lived.

- Record whether they are able to be still for any length of time, and, if so, in what circumstances? Are they able to listen to others relating an incident?

- Note the children's responses to the music stopping in a game. Are there any who don't seem to hear? Do they only react on seeing other children reacting? Who stops when the music stops but is slow to carry out the required response?

- Observations of children painting their portraits can often reveal how they feel about themselves, whether they are happy to be who they are. Note, for example, whether children with a darker skin colour themselves in a lighter tone. If children think they look better 'white', then this is saying something about their level of self-esteem.

- In games such as 'What's missing?', note the reactions of the children to becoming the centre of attention. Are they reticent to take a turn or very eager? Can they keep the secret as to what item has been removed, or do they have to tell the child whose turn it is?

- When playing games that require the children to move items silently, note which children are able to do this. Much will depend not only on their fine motor control but also on their ability to sit still and listen attentively. Note which children have the most acute hearing and how well they can pinpoint the direction of the sound. Note also who has the control to creep forward quietly and pick up the item with the minimum of sound.

- Note the children's reactions to having their feet washed. For some, this may be affirming; others may simply be taken up with the tickling effect; some children will not want to be touched so intimately, and this could indicate that they are on the autistic spectrum or have been abused in some way. However, assumptions should not be made from such isolated incidents, but they may alert staff to the need for closer observation of the child.

Effective practice

- Children need to be given the freedom to explore their interests and to make their own mistakes unless they are putting themselves, or others, at serious risk. Learning by our own mistakes is always more powerful than being told not to do something. Children need to know that the adult is available to provide support and to be a partner in their learning, to interact with them and to model care of the environment. Clearing up after an activity can be done together at first, but children should gradually be able to take over responsibility for this and be encouraged by having their efforts praised by the adult.

- Make sure that the children have the time and the opportunity to continue with an activity until they feel it is finished. Plenary times are very important and should not be regarded as an add-on if there is time available. By talking about their project, children can learn to express their thoughts in a logical manner, as they describe the process they have followed. Their way of doing things may not have been 'logical', but they must be given assurance that their way of problem-solving has been valid. This will encourage them to experiment again and to try new ways, perhaps more effective ways, of achieving their goal another time. The language used in reporting back will be more formal than the language used during an activity; indeed, this may have been minimal if they were working alone, but even in conversation with others, they would not have needed to name their materials or, necessarily, to speak in sentences.

- Model inclusive, respectful language and challenge any name-calling or bullying of any kind. Use one of the stories below, or a Persona Doll to explore why this is not acceptable. Encourage the children to respond positively to others and to begin to reflect on their own attitudes and actions. Help them to understand why it is important to listen to each other and to make sure that all the children have an opportunity to speak and to listen. Those who speak in a language other than English should have an opportunity to express themselves using that language, or to draw a picture, or to show by gesture what they feel. These children will eventually be able to use a noun and a verb in English, and this should be welcomed and fed back to them in a sentence, followed by a comment that seeks to extend the interaction. The children should not be expected to repeat the full version. Listening is tiring for anyone if they are struggling to understand what is being said, so keep such sessions short.

Planning and resourcing

- Always keep a ready supply of unbreakable mirrors and magnifying glasses for the children to explore parts of their own bodies and their environment. This type of resource should always be accessible to allow the children to follow up their interests.

- Provide a variety and range of materials and activities to stimulate the children's imagination and to encourage them to explore and experiment. They need to be able to make their own choices but should also be encouraged to work together with adults and their peers, so make sure that some activities need cooperation from others – for example, circle games and role play.

- Plan activities that are challenging for the children but not completely beyond their reach or else they may become unnecessarily frustrated and disheartened and, at worst, give up trying altogether. Respect a child's right as an individual to complete a task without being told to 'hurry up', or to 'tidy up now!'. Remember that a child may want to return to an activity later on and develop their project further. Provision should be made for this, even if it means keeping to one side a model that the child has constructed earlier.

- Help the children to learn to listen to others by holding short plenary sessions or letting a child say a rhyme or sing a song in their preferred language. Support materials should be provided if these would help the children to concentrate. For example, during a song, the other children could add a musical accompaniment.

Home links

- Activities such as those under meditation above will need permission from parents. The benefits may need to be explained and assurances given that this will not be connected to any particular religious faith, if that is of concern. Current research is discovering some fascinating links between meditation and emotional development for all of us; it is certainly well worth exploring. We may find that Pascal, the French philosopher, was right when he said that all the misfortunes of humankind derived from one single thing, which is people's inability to be still in a room.

- Exchange information with parents about their children's increasing independence and encourage them to give them time to share what they have achieved during the day. Stories can help to begin conversations about choices and ambitions. They will need the assurance of knowing there is 'only one of me' and that they are highly valued for who they are.

- Parents and carers need to feel accepted by setting staff. Their self-esteem will be communicated to their children and will enable them to learn to respect and value their culture and background and to seek out challenges with increased confidence.

Additional stories

Barkow, A. (2002) *Alfie's Angels,* London: Mantra Lingua. (This story deals with a gender issue: a little boy who wants to be an angel in the school show. Available in English and more than fifteen bilingual editions.)

Binch, C. (2005) *Silver Shoes,* London: Frances Lincoln. (Molly badly wants some silver shoes like the other girls when she goes to her first dance class, but her mum says she must wait and see if she likes it first. She finds this difficult to handle, especially as her best friend has a pair already.)

French, S. (2008) *What Will You Be?* London: Frances Lincoln. (At the school dressing-up parade, everyone has decided to go in the standard costumes, but Sasha is going to be different from the others, and even surprises himself.)

Hutchins, P. (2003) *There's Only One of ME!* London: Harper Collins. (A birthday party for a little girl is at first overwhelming because she is related in so many different ways to the various members of her extended family who have come to celebrate with her, but in the end she realises that it is best just to enjoy being the birthday girl.)

King, S. M. (2005) *Milli, Jack and the Dancing Cat,* London: Frances Lincoln. (Milli is afraid to show people what she loves to do, until she makes friends with Jack and the Dancing Cat. Then she experiences the joy of being herself and letting her imagination run riot.)

Lemmens, R. (2002) *A Box Full of Monsters,* London: Mantra Lingua. (Boris receives a parcel but he dares not open it because he is afraid of what it might contain. This is a story to help children cope with a fear of the unknown. Available in English and three bilingual editions.)

Monks, L. (2004) *I Wish I Were a Dog,* London: Egmont Press. (Kitty is fed up with being a cat; dogs seem to have far more fun. But then she realises that dogs cannot climb trees or catch mice, so perhaps being a cat is better after all. The message being that everyone is special just the way they are!)

—— (2007) *Aaaarrgghh, Spider!* London: Egmont Press. (Spider wants to be a pet, but he is always being thrown outside until one day the family are so impressed with the beautiful webs he has created in the garden that they decide he would make a good pet after all.)

Robert, N. B. (2002) *The Swirling Hijaab,* London: Mantra Lingua. (This is a gentle, wistful tale of a little Muslim girl's feelings for her headscarf. It is beautifully illustrated with a simple text. Available in English and more than ten bilingual editions.)

Ross, T. (2007) *I Want To Be,* London: HarperCollins. (The Little Princess tries to decide what she wants to be and considers being kind, loving, clean, good at smiling, healthy, clever, or tall).

Velthuijs, M. (2000) *Frog Is Frog,* London: Milet Publishing. (Frog is happy that he can jump and swim, until he sees the duck flying, the pig making cakes and the hare reading. Then he feels sad because he cannot do any of those things, but he soon learns that his friends love him for who he is. Available in English and bilingual editions.)

Persona Doll story

Introduce the Persona Doll over a number of sessions before talking about an issue.

Meet Millie

Millie is three years old, but nearly four. She is small for her age and has beautiful red hair. (*What colour is your hair?*) She lives with her mum in a small flat. (*What sort of house do you live in?*) They have a kitchen off the living room and two bedrooms and a bathroom. Mum sleeps in the bigger room, and Millie has the smaller one. It has just enough room for a single bed and a tiny wardrobe with drawers in. Millie likes her room; it is painted blue. (*Tell us about your room. Do you share with anyone else? What colour is it? What do you like about your room? Is there anything you don't*

Millie

like?) They live on the third floor, and Millie likes looking out of the window over the park opposite. She is too young to go to the park on her own; she sometimes goes with her mum but more often she goes with her grandpa who lives close by with her grandma. Grandma doesn't go out much because she gets out of breath. Mum said she used to smoke a lot when she was little, but she stopped when Mum started to get bad asthma. Millie's mum goes out to work in an office in town, and Millie goes to a day nursery, but she doesn't stay as long as some of the other children, because her grandpa picks her up every day at three o'clock and takes her home with him. Sometimes they stop in the park before going home for tea. Her mum takes her to nursery in the morning at eight o'clock and picks her up again from her grandma's at six o'clock. Her mum doesn't work on Saturday or Sunday, so she gets to see her more, and they usually go to the supermarket on Saturday morning. Otherwise, Saturday is a quiet day, but Millie doesn't mind. She likes just being with her mum at home. Mum cleans up a bit, and Millie plays in her room or watches television. Sometimes mum goes out with her friends on Saturday night, and then Millie stays at Grandma and Grandpa's for the night.

Millie has no brothers or sisters, and she doesn't have a dad; she doesn't know why, but she loves her grandpa, so that seems just as good. (*How many people are in your family? Do you have any brothers and sisters?*) She hasn't any friends in the flats, but she has a best friend at nursery called Sarah. (*Have you got a best friend?*) Sarah comes from a big family, and sometimes her mummy invites Millie to tea. They live in a terraced house round the corner from Millie's grandma and grandpa. Sarah only goes to the nursery in the afternoons, and Millie can't wait to see her every day. Sarah is taller than Millie and wears her hair in tiny black plaits. She has dark brown skin, and she laughs a lot. Millie always feels happy when she is with Sarah, and she loves playing with her brothers and sisters. Sarah has two brothers – Josh, who is seven, and Sol, who is five – and a baby sister, Becky, who is one. Sometimes Millie and Sarah help to give Becky her tea and play with her while her mummy runs her bath.

Millie's favourite food is pasta bake with tuna, and ice cream for afters. She can't have it every day, but she usually has it on Friday because that's the day she gets to choose. On Tuesdays she goes with Sarah to Tumble Tots. It is held in another room in the nursery so they can go themselves, and Grandpa picks them both up afterwards.

Millie's favourite game is dressing up. Sarah's mum makes clothes at home, and she always has lots of pieces of material that she lets the girls play with. Millie's house is very tidy, but Sarah's house is a rough and tumble place. Sarah's mum goes on about the mess sometimes but nothing really changes. (*Where do you play? What games do you like to play? Why?*)

Sarah has got a dad, but he works in a factory and Millie doesn't see him very often, as he comes home after six o'clock. Sarah's mum and dad were born in England but her nana and grandad came from a country called

Trinidad when they were little. They still have lots of family in Trinidad, and Sarah wants to go to see them, but her mum says it would cost too much money for them all to go. On Sunday, Sarah's family all go to the Pentecostal church on the corner of their street. Millie has sometimes heard the singing when she walks round to Grandpa and Grandma's for lunch with her mum on Sunday morning. It always sounds so exciting that Millie would love to have a look inside, but her mum says they cannot just open the door and stare in at people. Millie feels sure no one would mind, but she doesn't say so. They don't go to church, but Millie doesn't know why, and when she asks her mum, she just says, 'It's not our thing!' Millie thinks it might be her thing, and she wants to go and see one day. (*What do you do on Saturdays and Sundays?*)

Issue (example)

Sometimes, Millie gets a bit upset because one of the girls at the gym club, who's nearly six, calls her 'squirrel nut' because of her red hair, and if Sarah tells her to stop, she says Sarah looks dirty. Once, when she said that, Sarah pushed her over, and she got in trouble from the teacher, but Millie secretly thought she was very brave. (*What do you think Millie and Sarah feel like when that girl calls them names? Why does she call them names? What should they do about the girl?*)

 # The EYFS principles

The EYFS principles are grouped into four themes that are concerned with the individual needs of the child, the importance of building positive relationships and the need for the adults in the setting to create an environment that enables the child to learn and to develop to the best of their ability. As these themes relate to this section on dispositions and attitudes, the focus is on how the children become interested, excited and motivated about their learning. As an adult in the setting, you are in a very powerful position: you are physically bigger than the children; you have more experience of life; you know more; and you set the tone for the setting. Consider for a moment your own dispositions and attitudes. Are you are still interested in learning? To give yourself a health check, think back over the last five years. Ask yourself:

- Has your thinking developed?
- Have you learned something new?
- Have you moved on in any area of your life?

If you are no different now than you were five years ago, then either you are perfect, or you have stagnated. If you are still keen to learn, then your whole attitude to the children, to their parents and carers and to your colleagues will be creative and positive. You will not be assuming that you have all the answers, that your way is always best, that you know everything there is to know about child development, and the chances are that the children in your care will be stimulated to learn. They will sense your excitement, and that will motivate them to want to explore and to experiment. The model you provide of consideration and concern when listening to their parents and carers will teach them how to treat others, and your discussions with them about matters of fairness will help them to see why it is important not to hurt others or to make them feel inferior and useless. Your respect for their views and your support for their decision-making will empower them and enable them to be content with who they are and to investigate their environment with confidence.

Self-confidence and self-esteem

From birth–20 months

Development matters

- Seek to be looked at and approved of.

- Find comfort in touch and in the human face.

- Thrive when their emotional needs are met.

- Gain physical, psychological and emotional comfort from 'snuggling in'.

- Feel safe and secure within healthy relationships with key people.

- Sustain healthy emotional attachments through familiar, trusting, safe and secure relationships.

- Express their feelings within warm, mutual, affirmative relationships.

Key words

establish relationships, safety

Main story: *Dad Mine!*
(J. Kemp and C. Walters (2003) London: Frances Lincoln)

This story explores the relationships of a number of different creatures with their dads. A little boy discovers that, although some dads might be bigger or more colourful, his own dad is the best. There are many books about a close mother–child relationship, but it is good to have a number, like this one, that highlight a close and loving relationship between little children and their dads. Whatever relationship is highlighted in a story, there will be some children who either do not have one or other of their parents living with them, or whose parents are frightening people to be with. That is why it is always important to talk about someone special in the children's lives, to widen the possibilities in the follow-up discussion. The parallel story is *Mum Mine* (see below).

Activities

- Provide a baby gym in close proximity to familiar adults so that their voices can still be heard. The gym will be brightly coloured and have mobiles hanging overhead for babies to follow with their eyes, and buttons to press that set off gentle musical tunes or animal noises. At first, these buttons will be activated accidentally by babies or operated by the adult, but as babies gain more control over their limbs they will be able to deliberately play their own music. Tiny mirrors may be built into the mobiles to reflect the light, and the mat itself may be made of different materials that babies can explore. Some areas may be hidden under flaps, and, as babies develop they will be able to explore these for themselves. Small toys can be attached by Velcro and released for play; these can provide opportunities for babies to experience different textures that they can cuddle, pull, stroke, crumple and squeeze. All these things stimulate the baby's senses and attract the attention of familiar adults who, by their approval, boost the baby's sense of self-worth and confidence.

- Make sure that a special item of comfort is available for babies to snuggle up to when you are otherwise engaged in making preparations for a meal or a nappy change. This item might be something brought from home, such as a piece of muslin or a soft toy. In this case, the item will need to be kept in a special place so that the child is not caused distress by another child walking off with it.

- When you cannot give babies direct contact, make sure you keep talking to them and singing familiar songs and rhymes, so that they do not feel forgotten. It may be that times can be set aside for older siblings to come and play with them, and as they get older, they will begin to interact with other children for longer periods of time.

- Being able to choose and handle books on their own will give children a sense of independence and the confidence to enjoy books, secure that they know what will happen in the story. As they begin to act out their ideas and feelings in imaginative play, they will develop positive attitudes towards themselves and other people. However, this is not to decry the fact that they will still frequently need times to snuggle up close and share a book with a key adult.

Look, listen and note

- Take note of how babies respond to the adult's attention. Do they make eye contact? Do they utilise their arms and legs? How do they respond when they feel abandoned by the adult? Is any particular adult more important than another? How do they respond to the attentions of other children? Do they recognise their own brothers and sisters? Can you tell by their reactions?

- Observe the babies' progress in playing on their own and their increasing ability to make choices. When did the uncontrolled arm action that triggered a musical toy become a deliberate movement to produce the desired sounds? Do they have a favourite song that they are able to activate?

- Record the babies' developing language as they move from contented early gurgling and experimental shrieks when their needs have been met to more controlled words and actions to portray their changing moods. Can you decipher their feelings from their gestures and early communication?

- Note objects that the baby is particularly drawn to when they are beginning to feel tired, or lonely, and the particular company they seek at such times. Is a comforter still tucked under the arm of the young child as they snuggle in for a story?

Effective practice

- The provision of playthings such as a baby gym provides stimulation for babies and sets challenges, but they should not feel abandoned, even if the adult takes the opportunity to prepare some food or get ready for a nappy change. They will need frequent assurances that someone is nearby and need to hear their voice.

- A comforter brought from home needs to be kept apart for each baby's sole use. A setting item that becomes a particular favourite might still be made available at particular times of the day, but at other times may well be played with by other children; this will help the child to gradually get used to the idea of sharing and thinking about the feelings of other people.

Planning and resourcing

- Provide equipment such as a baby gym with musical and tactile stimulation that will motivate the babies to explore on their own and to become confident in their own abilities.

- Provide some large comfy chairs and sofas in the book corner, where adults and children can snuggle up to share a story. This frequent reassurance that they are valued and loved as a person in their own right is very important for young children's emotional well-being and supports them in developing positive relationships. The provision of an environment that enables the child to experience a healthy balance between activity and quiet time is crucial for the child's continuing learning and development.

Home links

- Feelings are particularly difficult to express in an additional language, and parents might be reticent about trying to share these with a third party. Those who are refugees or asylum-seekers may find this particularly difficult for a number of reasons. They are likely to be traumatised by atrocities committed against their family in their own country and might feel less than secure in their new surroundings. They may want to keep a low profile and be afraid of sharing too many details about themselves in case information is passed on to the authorities and they are deported. Other parents may simply have had a bad experience of school themselves and their own confidence needs boosting.

- Patience will be needed to make sure that parents and carers are comfortable with the routines and treatment of their children. Items taken for granted in this country such as rattles and strings of beads for prams are cultural and might be new to some parents and carers. Share the benefits of such items and demonstrate the fun their child has with the baby gym, but also be willing to receive ideas from them and to incorporate these into your own routines, where appropriate. More serious concerns about feeding, rest and behaviour management will be considered elsewhere.

Additional stories

- Aigner-Clark, J. (2004) *See How I Feel*, New York: Hyperion Books for Children. (Children are able to make excited, sad, happy, proud, silly, or angry faces using a mirror.)

- Inkpen, M. (2006) *Wibbly Pig is Happy*, London: Hodder Children's Books. (Also shows Wiggly being busy, surprised and upset, with his dog giving him a big lick at the end to try to cheer him up. Board book.)

- Kemp, J. and Walters, C. (2003) *Mum Mine*, London: Frances Lincoln. (A celebration of the mother–child relationship across the animal kingdom and a little boy's conviction that his mum is best.)

Monjo, J. and Monjo, F. N. (2003) *Three Kinds of Scared,* London: Frances Lincoln. (Marty Muskrat is scared of riding bikes, climbing trees and swinging on ropes, but his friends help him to discover that there are only three ways of being scared and show him that he can deal with them all.)

Smee, N. (2006) *Funny Face With Other,* London: Bloomsbury. (Lots of expressions of feelings to copy with a space in the middle for a photograph of the baby to personalise it, with a mirror opposite to make faces in. In the setting situation, a picture of one of the babies could be used with permission from their parents or carers, or an anonymous baby. Board book.)

Stoppard, M. (2007) *Happy Baby,* London: Dorling Kindersley. (This book shows a baby being happy, sad, grumpy or excited. Baby Board book.)

From 16–36 months

Development matters

- Make choices that involve challenge, when adults ensure their safety.

- Explore from the security of a close relationship with a caring and responsive adult.

- Develop confidence in own abilities.

- Begin to be assertive and self-assured when others have realistic expectations of their competence.

- Begin to recognise danger and know whom to turn to for help.

- Feel pride in their own achievements.

Key words

challenging choices, pride in achievement

Main story: *I Have Feelings!*
(L. Novotny-Hunter (2002) Frances Lincoln, London)

As children develop personally and socially, their emotional development will become more apparent to them and they will come to recognise that they have feelings and that they need others to understand what these are. Sometimes these feelings will be influenced by how they are feeling at a particular moment, or a need they have. At other times, they are to do with the kind of characteristics they are developing, what their preferences are and what they are interested in. We all need to feel that we are special in our own way and need to take pride in learning new skills, but at this age feelings can sometimes be frightening. This simple little story is not about extreme emotion but follows a little mouse through his day. It begins with his waking up, which he says is his best time, because then he feels happy. Later, when he goes to the park with his family, he starts to feel really excited. But when his baby sister gets a turn on the swing before he does, he starts to feel jealous. These feelings will be becoming familiar to the children, and they need adults who are willing to talk to them about them and to reassure them that we all 'have feelings'.

Activities

- Children can be involved in the provision of snacks, providing they are properly supervised. They can use knives, for example, to cut up fruit. The knives obviously should have rounded ends and not be very sharp, but children can be involved in this kind of activity if they are taught how to use their tools safely.

- Climbing apparatus that challenges the children should also be available. I was saddened recently on visiting a nursery with a wonderful outdoor area, with lots of mature trees, to learn that the staff had been ordered by the Council to trim off all the lower branches so that the children could not climb them. My thoughts turned to the happy hours my brother and I spent astride a low bough of an ancient tree, pretending we were riding a horse.

- Provide spoons, whisks, pots and pans as well as commercially produced instruments from around the world for the children to explore.

They will be able to discover and repeat noisy and quiet sounds, and it will help them to connect to the rhythms of life around them.

- Provide various kinds of treasure boxes. The items should be selected to stimulate the senses and to encourage independent play within a supportive environment. One box could contain natural items, for example, objects made from natural materials, such as wood, jute, metal, wool, cotton, velvet or silk. Also, include herbs of various kinds, conkers and cones. Another box could contain objects that can roll, for example, small rolling pins, cotton reels, balls of various sizes, fruit and vegetables such as oranges, lemons, turnips and carrots, as well as vehicles with wheels. A third could contain strips of material, ribbons and scarves of various lengths, sizes and shapes, some of which could be gently perfumed, which can be scrunched or waved. The boxes must be fairly sturdy, and the items need to be changed from time to time to maintain high levels of interest, but not so often that children cannot spend enough time finding and playing with their favourite things and practising the various movements. If the items are washable, then this will need to be attended to regularly. If they are natural materials, such as conkers, cones or herb leaves, then these will need to be replaced. This play should be supervised but there should be no adult intervention unless the child is in danger. Babies can participate in this activity, although if they are unable to sit unaided, they will need support in the form of cushions.

 ## Look, listen and note

- Note how the children manipulate tools; it provides not only a good opportunity to access the development of their fine motor skills, but also how confident they are in their own abilities and whether they know where to go to for guidance if they are unsure.

- Observe the children climbing and pushing themselves to their physical limits. Do they take calculated risks? Are they assured of their own skills and ready to learn new ones? Are they able to engage in pretence through their play and use this as a way of expressing their feelings?

- Playing alone with a treasure box or with a set of 'instruments' will provide a good opportunity for the practitioner to observe the progress of children in terms of their curiosity, their confidence to explore and their response to new experiences.

Effective practice

- Children need challenges, whether it is in terms of testing their own feelings and responding to others, or whether it is in terms of their physical development and discovering who they are and what they can achieve. Health-and-safety issues are very important, but they must not paralyse the setting staff so that challenging activities are not provided.

- Music-making or exploring a treasure box with a supportive adult offering encouragement and showing approval will help children to gain the assurance and the confidence to see what they can do on their own and also to enjoy the security of a close relationship.

Planning and resourcing

- Have photographs displayed of all the staff so that the children, the parents and carers – and indeed any visitor to the setting – can clearly identify those responsible for the care of the children.

- Have ready-made pictures of all the activities in the setting, so that all the children, regardless of their abilities or disabilities, can convey their choices. Consider the way these are presented so that children who are visually impaired can be given the maximum assistance. Take advice from their support teachers; it is not always the size that matters as much as the clarity of the visuals and the text.

- Provide plenty of outdoor opportunities for children to develop their skills in the natural environment, as well as using ordinary materials indoors. Commercial toys have their place, but expensive equipment is not always needed: a fir cone, a spoon, a pot and a silk square can excite the imagination and the senses just as effectively, if not more so.

Home links

Many of these activities involve everyday objects which are easily provided at home, and there can be a fruitful exchange of ideas and reports of observed behaviour. What the child has achieved at home needs to be recorded and celebrated in the setting, too, and vice versa.

Additional stories

Alborough, J. (2003) *Some Dogs Do,* Cambridge Mass.: Candlewick Press. (Dogs can walk and jump, but they don't usually fly. This one does, however, but only when he is feeling really happy.)

Anholt, C. and Anholt, L. (2005) *Going to Playgroup,* Danbury: Orchard Books. (This story explores the fun of starting playgroup, which should help to allay any fears for those about embark on this new adventure.)

Cabrera, J. (2008) *If You're Happy and You Know It,* London: Gullane Children's Books. (An interactive adventure in the forest with characters such as the cheeky Monkey and the enormous Elephant.)

Coplestone, L. and Coplestone, J. (2005) *Noah's Bed,* London: Frances Lincoln. (On the ark, Noah's grandson is frightened by a thunderstorm and creeps into his grandparents' bed, only to find that he is not alone in seeking comfort from the storm.)

Harter, D. (2001) *Walking through the Jungle,* London: Mantra Lingua. (A little girl heads off into the forest, crosses a desert, climbs over icebergs and, in spite of the creatures hiding behind the trees, makes it home safe and sound in time for tea. Available in English and more than ten bilingual editions.)

Noble, S. (2001) *Uh Oh!* Slough: Zero to Ten. (A little girl begins her first day at nursery rather tentatively. As the day progresses, she gradually becomes more confident until her dad picks her up.)

Novotny-Hunter, J. (2007) *I Can Do It!* London: Frances Lincoln. (Little Guinea Pig goes to nursery where he can be fast, strong, quiet, busy, careful, noisy, clever and helpful.)

Roddie, S. (2007) *Colour Me Happy!* London: Macmillan Children's Books. (Little Tiger and his friends know about being happy, sad, funny, dreamy and glad. They will be able to help the children express their feelings.)

Ross, T. (2008) *I Want My Light On!* London: Andersen Press. (Little Princess is not so much afraid of the dark as of ghosts. Everyone is clear that ghosts don't exist, but then what's that under her bed?)

From 30–60+ months

Development matters

- Show increasing confidence in new situations.

- Talk freely about their home and community.

- Take pleasure in gaining more complex skills.

- Have a sense of personal identity.

- Express needs and feelings in appropriate ways.

- Have an awareness and pride in self as having own identity and abilities.

Early learning goals

- Respond to significant experiences, showing a range of feelings when appropriate.

- Have a developing awareness of their own needs, views and feelings, and be sensitive to the needs, views and feelings of others.

- Have a developing respect for their own cultures and beliefs and those of other people.

Key words

personal identity, home and community, mutual respect

Main story: *Little Owl*
**(P. Harper (2003), Macmillan Children's Books, London,
a soft-to-touch book)**

Little Owl practised flapping his wings every night so that they would grow strong enough for him to fly. When he is inspired by his friends to explore some new places, his mummy agrees and they fly together. But when Little Owl gets scared and misses the safety of his tree, he asks to go home, and his mummy agrees saying that he had been 'a very brave owl indeed'. Little Owl didn't feel very brave and when Bat came and asked him to play races, he began to worry that he was not up to it. But Mummy Owl said he was a big owl now so he puffed out his chest and flapped his wings really hard. If his mummy thought he could do it, then it must be true, and after a shaky start he discovered that he really could fly on his own. He flew back to the nest and was so excited at his achievement. 'I knew you could', said Mummy Owl and told him that he was big and strong and very, very brave, as she hugged him tight.

This is a lovely story of developing independence and one to which small children can relate as they take their own first steps, albeit still under the watchful eye of their parents and carers. It also has a message for the adults. The mother owl was very supportive and encouraging but was always helping Little Owl to take the next step and in no sense held him back. Nevertheless, she was still waiting for him at home to give him a hug and inspire him with new confidence for his next challenge.

Activities

Facial expressions displaying emotions

- Produce a set of twenty-four cards showing six different emotions for the children to identify. Have four different children showing the same emotion. If you use different characters displaying a similar emotion, it could be useful later on when you want to talk about different ways of showing the same feeling and the range of intensity that exists in any one emotion. These may be commercially produced pictures designed for this purpose, magazine pictures or your own photographs. Begin with the 'happy' and 'sad' cards. Ask the children, 'Is this girl *happy* or *sad*? What do you think has happened?' Then move on to the 'angry' and 'scared' pictures. Ask the children, 'Is this boy angry about something?' 'Is he scared?' 'How do you know?' Eventually, you can move on to 'excited' and 'surprised'.

- You may have a set of lotto cards showing children displaying different emotions that you can use for this exercise as a preparation for playing the game. Ask the children to sort the pictures into groups based on the feelings they are displaying. See if the children can identify the pictures portraying similar emotions and ask them to describe the children and what is happening to them in their own words and make a note of the words they use. Build up a word bank of terms used for a person who is, for example, sad.

- Use some unbreakable hand-held mirrors so the children can imitate the different expressions in a mirror. You can model this first and ask the children to identify the changing expressions on your face as you look sad, happy, surprised and angry. Have the mirrors placed somewhere accessible so that the children can use them any time they want to experiment on their own or with a friend.

- Ask the children to think of one thing that makes them happy, sad, angry, scared, excited or surprised. They might want to use the formula, 'I feel happy when …'

- Play 'True or False'. Show one of the pictures and say, 'This boy is excited. Do you agree? Yes or No?' The children can run to an area labelled 'Yes' or 'No', perhaps a chalked circle on the ground, or a hoop. Allow the children to explain the choice they have made; sometimes they may have a plausible explanation for a surprising answer.

● An additional set of twenty-four cards can be produced with a simple round shape on each to represent a face showing, very simply, six different emotions. For example, there might be six sets of happy, sad, angry, scared, surprised and excited faces. These can be used for a number of activities:

  ● A game of snap. When two cards are turned up that are the same, the child who shouts 'snap' can talk about the feeling represented.

  ● A game of pelmanism where twelve identical pairs of cards are spread out face down on the table or the floor and the children take turns to look at two cards and try to find a matching pair. If the two cards are not the same, they must be turned back over and replaced in the same position. If they are a pair, the child keeps the set and describes the emotion represented. This involves the children watching which cards the other children have turned up and remembering where they are, if they are to be successful.

  ● Regularly, sit a small group of children on chairs in a circle facing inwards and place four cards representing different emotions (build up to six) face up on the floor and ask the children to pick one up, in turn, to show how they are feeling at that moment, and to explain why.

  ● Play a 'Simon Says' type of game using feelings – Simon says, 'Be sad' (or angry, happy, scared, etc.) – or get the children to take turns to choose a feeling, then everyone shows that feeling on their face. When the children are ready, introduce the different range of intensity a feeling can have such as cross, angry and furious.

● Discuss the different types of words we use to describe feelings. Children may feel more than sad, and they need to know the words to express this such as 'disappointed', 'miserable', 'confused' or 'upset'. At first, the adult needs to model these words to build up the children's emotional literacy.

- Use face masks with different emotions on either side as a visual aid for use in a story, or puppets displaying separate feelings according to which way round they are held. These can then be made available for the children to use in their role play.

Look, listen and note

- Take note of which children are able to communicate their needs and who is uncertain about what they have been asked to do and always follow someone they think will know.

- Observe the children during imaginative play and see if they are able to use the words they have learned in the above activities to express their feelings and to give an explanation for the way they are feeling.

- Look for examples that demonstrate whether the children are aware of themselves as people with views and opinions that they are willing to express, and that indicate their level of self-esteem. Do they show a pride in their family and their background? Are they aware that other children are different and able to respect their beliefs and feelings? Do they attempt to stand up for another child who is being bullied, or try to comfort a child who is upset?

Effective practice

- Always keep the children's options open as far as possible, so they can make their own choices, while providing stimulating and challenging materials.

- If children get accustomed to talk about their feelings in this kind of enabling environment, a place of safety, this will help them to not bottle up their emotions and to not be afraid to share feelings of which they might otherwise feel ashamed. The fact that other people admit to being upset or jealous will help the children to ask for help and to move on. It is important that they learn to appreciate that the adults are there to support their learning. The children will need help in understanding that they can feel both upset and mad about something at the same time. The adults also need to acknowledge the children's feelings and to let them know that it is all right, for example, to feel sad or angry and that it usually helps to talk about it. They can help the children to understand why they have responded in a particular way to a situation. Stories can help here to open up the discussion and help the children to explore their own feelings through the eyes of someone else.

Planning and resourcing

- Plan time for the card games and circle activities outlined above. Think carefully about how you ask the children to form a circle. Sometimes issues arise around holding hands with others. A child might be rejected because they have severe eczema or because their skin tone is darker than the other children. These matters must be addressed but need to be sensitively handled, and it may be that the children are asked to form a circle in another way initially. They could sit on, or hold, the edge of a round table cloth, or hold a piece of coloured plaited string, elastic or rope that has been joined to make a circle. This is not to avoid addressing the issue but to avoid a child being hurt if you sense there might be an issue before you have had time to help the children reflect on such matters through the stories.

- Plan additional time to support children who are facing significant changes in their lives. They may have a new baby in the family, be moving house, be moving on if they are a traveller family, be going into hospital, transferring to a new stage in their schooling, experiencing the death of a close family member. Sadly, some children live continually in a state of uncertainty and fear. Some come from abusive homes; others face numerous operations; while others are unsure what has happened to their family and might themselves be moved or deported at a moment's notice.

- Provide role-play areas that reflect the diversity of our country, particularly if you are living in a monocultural area.

- Use Persona Dolls and other stories to introduce the children to those of other cultures, or those who are in some way different from them; otherwise, they are likely to feel afraid of difference and could become xenophobic. You will need to do some research yourself if you do not have direct access to those from the particular culture that you want to introduce. You will need to be able to explain why people do things differently and discuss this with the children. Use some of the books and websites at the back of this book.

Home links

Encourage parents to share stories with their children about feelings. Affirm that it is good to be open about their own emotions and to give their children space to explore and share how they are feeling, at their own pace, and in their own way. Parents and carers who speak English as an additional language will find such talk easier in their first language and should be encouraged to express themselves in this way.

Additional stories

Allen, J. (2008) *I'm Not Scared*, London: Frances Lincoln. (When Baby Owl is out at night in the woods, all the other animals keep telling him not to be scared. They don't seem to realise that owls are meant to go out at night, and that he's not scared!)

Ashley, B. (2002) *Clever Sticks*, London: Picture Lions. (Ling Sung doesn't like going to school because all the other children can do things that he can't, but one day he does something that makes everyone stare in amazement. At snack time, he uses two paintbrushes as chopsticks to pick up biscuits. This was something no one else could do, not even the teacher, and that made Ling Sung feel much more confident.)

Bradman, T. (1998) *It Came from Outer Space,* London: Mantra Lingua. (The children in a classroom are horrified when a space-craft lands on their school roof and an ugly monster comes out, but the monster seems friendly and shows them round its space-ship. The strange thing is the alien turns out to be a human being. Available in English and a few bilingual editions.)

Brownjohn, E. (2004) *All Kinds of Feelings,* London: Mantra Lingua. (This lift-the-flap book carries the message that it's important to accept your feelings, to trust them and to share them with others. Available in English and more than ten bilingual editions.)

Bryant-Mole, K. (1999) *I'm Happy,* London: Hodder Wayland. (Cartoons and humorous situations are used to help young children understand what it means to be happy.)

—— (1999) *I'm Shy,* London: Hodder Wayland. (Cartoons and humorous situations are used to help young children cope with being shy.)

Edwards, P. D. (2007) *I'm Big Enough Now!* London: Macmillan Children's Books. (A baby elephant thinks she is big enough to go to the lake and to the village on her own but soon discovers that she is much happier doing things with her mum, and she would wait until she was a bit bigger before exploring again on her own.)

Edwards, R. (2007) *Little Monkey's One Safe Place,* London: Frances Lincoln. (Scared by a storm, Little Monkey runs to his mother's arms. She tells him that he has always got one safe place, but he does not know what she means and goes off to try and find it.)

Genechten, G. V. (1999) *Floppy,* London: Mantra Lingua. (Floppy has one ear that will not stand up straight on its own. He tries to hide it and then to hold it up straight by tying a balloon to it, but the other rabbits laugh even more. In the end, he realises that we don't all have to be the same and that his friends love him for who he is. Available in English and more than twenty bilingual editions.)

—— (2002) *Floppy in the Dark,* London: Mantra Lingua. (This tackles fear of the dark when Floppy goes off to sleep in a tent on his own overnight and is scared by the noises he hears. Available in English and more than fifteen bilingual editions.)

Hall, A. (2008) *Fine As We Are,* London: Frances Lincoln. (Little Frog lives happily with his mum until the arrival of a large number of brothers and sisters. Sibling rivalry explored.)

Hambleton, L. (2001) *I'm Afraid Too!* London: Mantra Lingua. (A story about new experiences and being scared. The little wooden man lives in a pine tree until one day it is cut down and he is forced to explore new places further afield. What will he find there? Available in English and more than ten bilingual editions.)

McKinlay, P. (1998) *Elephants Don't Do Ballet,* London: Frances Lincoln. (Esmeralda is determined to join a ballet class, and, at first, the results are disastrous, but she soon confounds the sceptics and proves that it is possible for elephants to do ballet.)

Mennen, I. (2004) *One Round Moon and a Star for Me,* London: Frances Lincoln. (A young African boy watches a star falling for the birth of a new baby in his family. He needs reassurance that he still has a place, and he is still his papa's son.)

Mills, D. (2002) *Sam's First Day,* London: Mantra Lingua. (Although he loves to talk, on his first day at school, Sam stopped talking. He enjoyed playing games and reading, but he wouldn't talk. Available in English and more than ten bilingual editions.)

Mitchell, P. (2007) *Petar's Song,* London: Frances Lincoln. (Petar has to escape from his home with his mother and brother when war breaks out, leaving his father in the village with the other men. He is so sad that he cannot play his violin anymore until one day a song of peace and new beginnings comes into his head. For children aged from five to eight years.)

Moodie, F. (2008) *Noko and the Night Monster,* London: Frances Lincoln. (Every night, Takudu the Aardvark shivers and shakes because he is afraid of the Night Monster. In the end, Noko the Porcupine sets off to try and find a cure for his friend.)

Moroney, T. (2005) *When I'm Feeling Happy,* Bath: The Five Mile Press. (Helps children to feel comfortable with different emotions when they have little experience of life and may have a limited ability to be able to express those feelings.)

(📖) —— (2005) *When I'm Feeling Sad,* Bath: The Five Mile Press. (See above.)

(📖) Moses, B. (1994) *I Feel Frightened,* London: Hodder Wayland. (Useful for talking about why people get frightened and what they can do about it.)

(📖) —— (1994) *I Feel Sad,* London: Hodder Wayland. (Useful for discussion about why people feel sad and whether they can or should do anything about it.)

(📖) —— (1997) *I'm Worried,* London: Hodder Wayland. (Useful for talking about why people get worried and what they can do about it.)

(📖) Moss, M. (2005) *Jungle Song,* London: Frances Lincoln. (Little Tapir is lured into the jungle by the music of the creatures: spiders, monkeys, firebirds, snakes and insects all have their own rhythms. However, when the beat stops, Little Tapir finds himself all alone, and he doesn't feel as brave. He realises how dangerous the jungle can be, and he is very glad when his mother comes to find him.)

(📖) Pitcher, C. (2005) *The Winter Dragon,* London: Frances Lincoln. (Rory is afraid of the winter darkness until the dragon he made comes alive and tells him tales of dinosaurs and crocodiles, of knights and battles, and soon Rory is feeling much braver.)

(📖) Robertson, M. P. (2008) *Big Brave Brian,* London: Frances Lincoln. (Brian is the bravest man in the world; he is not afraid of monsters, giants or things that go bump in the night, but there is one thing he is afraid of! Available in English and more than five bilingual editions.)

Persona Doll story

Introduce the Persona Doll over a number of sessions, but in this case there might need to be some discussion of issues as you go along because of Martin's hearing impairment.

Meet Martin

Martin is five years old. He lives with his mummy and daddy and older sister, Emma, who is eight years old. They live in a house on its own – called a detached house – and Emma and Martin each have their own bedroom. (*Do you have a bedroom of your own, or do you share?*) Their mum is a doctor, and their dad is a nurse. Their dad works in a hospital, so he sometimes has to work at night, but their mum only works in the daytime for four days a week. The children live opposite to the school, so they just have to walk over the road to get there, although there is a lollipop man to help them cross safely. (*Do you have someone to help you cross the road?*) They are very lucky because when they get home from school, either Mum or Dad is always there, sometimes both.

When Martin was born, he couldn't hear very well; sometimes he has a ringing sound in his head. He wears hearing aids, and these help him a little bit. He is learning to understand what people say by watching their lips moving, and he also uses a special sign language. He can talk, but he cannot hear himself very well, and it is difficult for other people to understand what he is saying. His mummy and daddy and sister can usually understand him, and they have learned to sign, too, so that Martin can let them know what he wants without getting too upset. Sometimes he does get cross if Emma is playing with her friend, Mimi, and won't let him play. He screams very loudly, and she gets mad with him and slams the door of her room. (*What do you think Martin feels like when he screams? What do you think Emma is feeling when she slams the door? What do you think happens after this?*)

Martin goes to the same school as Emma. She is in Year Three, but Martin goes to the partially hearing unit in the school and has most of his lessons there. He does join in some lessons with the other children, mostly for games and free-choice afternoons. He usually enjoys that, although he is still rather nervous. He worries in case he can't understand what the teacher says, or in case the other children will not be able to understand what *he* says. His class teacher is usually very careful to turn towards Martin when he speaks to him, and to speak clearly, but he sometimes forgets. Mr Bonnet has taught all the children some signs, so they can speak to Martin. Most of the children enjoy this, although he still finds it difficult to make real friends, and there are two boys who always make fun of him in the playground and copy the way he speaks. (*How do you think Martin feels when they do that? What could he do about it?*)

Martin

Martin loves to play football with the boys and girls in his class, but he cannot hear when they shout instructions to him. He has to watch the other children very carefully and stop when they stop, or else he gets into trouble, because not everyone remembers that he can't hear.

Emma likes to play football, too, and sometimes they play together in their back garden. They have a goal net set up, and they take it in turns to be in goal and to shoot penalties. Sometimes Martin wins, and sometimes Emma does. (*Which games do you like to play?*)

Martin and Emma have a rabbit and two white mice to look after. They take it in turns to feed them and to clean them out. Martin loves to stroke the soft fur of the rabbit and to watch the mice playing in their cage. Sometimes he lets them run up his sleeve and they tickle the back of his neck. When they go on holiday, Mimi looks after them, and they look after her hamster when she goes on holiday. (*What pets do you have? How do you look after them? What do they like to eat? What do they feel like when you hold them?*)

Martin's favourite food is sausage, chips and beans, but he does like to eat fruit as well, especially apples. They have an apple tree in their garden. They pick the apples every September and store them in boxes in the shed, so they always have plenty to eat. (*Can you tell Martin which other food is good for him to eat? What do you bring in your lunchbox?*)

Martin's dad is teaching him to play chess. (*Does anyone know what chess is? I've brought a board and some pieces to show you.*) Emma plays already and goes to the school club. Sometimes Martin goes with her to watch. He likes it in the chess club because it is quiet. Everyone is thinking hard, and they don't need to speak very much. It makes him feel the same as everyone else. He wants to join the club as soon as he can. He keeps practising very hard and plays against Emma and against his dad, but he cannot beat them yet.

On Saturday morning, they all go swimming. Mum is a really good swimmer, and she is teaching Martin. There is a teacher at the pool who can sign, and Mum hopes that Martin will soon feel brave enough to have proper lessons. He gets very anxious in the water, and it always seems to him that there is a strange booming sound in the swimming baths. Although he can take a few strokes on his own, he soon panics and starts to go under and shouts for Mum. Dad and Emma enjoy playing on the floats and the inflatables at the deep end. Emma can swim well, but Dad still watches her carefully. (*Do you go to the swimming baths? What does it smell like? Do you think it is noisy? What does it feel like in the water? Do you think it's fun, or do you get scared sometimes?*)

Martin would like to come and see you sometimes, if that's all right with you. He would like to teach you some signs so you can tell him what you've been doing. (*Would you like him to come to see you now and again and tell you what he's been doing and to find out what you've being doing? He wants you to think about how he can make some friends. He feels he's not really good at anything, so no one will want to be his friend. Do you think that's right? Perhaps you can give him some ideas next time he comes.*)

The EYFS principles

The EYFS principles are grouped into four themes which are concerned with the individual needs of the child, the importance of building positive relationships and the need for the adults in the setting to create an environment that enables the child to learn and to develop to the best of their ability. As these themes relate to this section on self-confidence and self-esteem, the focus is on how children develop a sense of their own value and learn to be sensitive to the significant events in their own lives and in the lives of other people. The degree to which we all, adults and children, feel good about ourselves is a major factor in how we act personally, socially and emotionally. As a general rule, it is easier to empathise with someone else and to reach out to support them when we feel comfortable about who we are, where we come from, whom we belong to. We are operating then from a position of strength, of confidence and self-assurance. This includes being realistic about our capabilities, our skills and our achievements, while not allowing that to stop us from continuing to learn and to develop. However, if one of our aims is to become a compassionate and generous person, and we want to pass on this ideal to the children we teach, then we must come to terms, at some point, with risk-taking. We are all aware of having to draw up risk assessments for activities within and without the setting, and this should not be ignored, but neither should they make us so cautious that the children are overprotected and are prevented from becoming the robust, independent people they are meant to be – people of inner strength, courageous in spirit and sensitive to those around them.

Making relationships

Birth-20 months

Development matters

- Enjoy the company of others and are sociable from birth.
- Depend on close attachments with a special person within their setting.
- Learn by interacting with others.
- Seek to gain attention in a variety of ways, drawing others into social interaction.
- Use their developing physical skills to make social contact.
- Build relationships with special people.

Key words

social development, build relationships

Main story: *So Much*
(Cooke, T. (2008), London: Walker Books)

Set in an African-Caribbean home, the baby waits with Mum as various members of the family arrive for a surprise party for Daddy. The baby becomes the centre of attention: Auntie Bidda wants to squeeze him; Uncle Didi wants to kiss him; Nannie and Gran-Gran want to eat him; Cousin Kay-Kay wants to fight him. When Daddy arrives home, the party can begin, and they all have a good time. The text will be too much for babies, but the pictures are big and colourful, and you can perform all the actions with the babies as you tell this action-packed story. You can squeeze and kiss them, pretend to eat and to fight them, all so they know that they are loved *so much,* just like the baby in the story.

Activities

- Develop a routine for greeting and saying goodbye to babies and their carers at the beginning and end of each session. It could be a simple, 'Hello Lee, how are you today?', 'Hello, Mrs Williams [or Lesley, if you are on first-name terms, and this has been agreed], how are you? Has Lee had a good night?', 'Bye bye, Lee, goodbye Mrs Williams. See you tomorrow.' For those for whom English is not their first language, learn an informal greeting and goodbye in the family's first language. This will help to ease the transition from home to the setting and vice versa for the children and their carers.

- Make sure that each baby has some one-to-one time with a key adult for interactive games such as 'Peep-boo'. Gently move the children's feet to mimic running, and their hands to mimic clapping. Make eye contact and, while talking and smiling, encourage a response from the babies by gently chucking them under the chin or patting their cheek with your finger. Little traditional rhyme or nonsense couplets can be employed to help you keep the 'conversation' going. The babies will soon recognise the sound of your voice, and this needs to be reassuring, especially if the sounds you make are unfamiliar and your intonation is different from that of the primary carer at home. Learn some simple rhymes or songs in the babies' first languages if they are unfamiliar with English sounds. As the babies become toddlers, they will be able to join in with the rhymes and songs, and individual help with the actions will enrich their close relationship with you as their key person.

- Key carers in the setting need to spend time talking with the children about their home and showing that they value their family structure, however that is constituted. Photographs of the different members of the family engaged in everyday and special events will help to stimulate the conversation. Children who need encouragement to speak because they are learning English, who are very shy or have speech and language difficulties, will often respond to a photograph, a puppet or a Persona Doll when they would find a direct face-to-face encounter with an adult, or even another child, much more difficult.

Look, listen and note

- During interactive games, note the ways in which the babies respond to you. What parts of their body are active? Do they copy your expressions and actions?

- Note how toddlers begin to respond to other adults and children, whether they bring 'offerings' in the form of, for example, a building block that they have been playing with or a pen of yours that has rolled onto the floor.

Effective practice

- Knowledge of the children's family background and culture is very important, as is information about their experience of languages. The children may begin to use sounds that are unfamiliar to you, and yet are the first words of their first language and need to be acknowledged as such.

- Making a strong relationship with their primary carers in the setting is the first priority for the children, and the ethos that they experience must be one that helps them to relax, feel nurtured and valued as a person in their own right.

- Early 'conversations' should focus on people and things that are familiar to the children. Photographs of home and family can often help to bridge the gap between the setting and the home and motivate the children to talk about the relationships they have with other children and adults.

Planning and resourcing

- How comings and goings are managed is vitally important in the setting if the handover of the children is to be smooth, with as little unnecessary stress as possible. These times must be discussed by the staff, planned for and reviewed regularly.

- Provision must be made to display the photographs of the children with their family in the home and with their carers and friends in the setting. This can take the form of an on-going wall collage, an album or a personal book created in the setting.

Home links

- Parents and carers can teach the staff to say 'hello' and 'bye bye' in the children's first languages and then be invited to reproduce these greetings and goodbyes so these can form part of a welcome poster.

- Parents and carers can also introduce the staff to simple rhymes and songs in their first language. These can be taped for all the children to listen to in the setting and to provide a reminder for the staff.

- Practitioners might need to reassure parents that the use of their baby's first language is crucial if they are to become bilingual and that they need have no fears that their child will not learn English; rather, it is their first language that will be vulnerable.

Additional stories

Alborough, J. (2005) *Hug*, Cambridge, Mass.: Candlewick Press. (A little chimpanzee sees that all the other animals in the forest have someone to hug, and he becomes more and more distressed until at last he hears his mum call, 'Bobo', and finds that he, too, has someone to hug. 'Hug' and 'Bobo' are the only words spoken in the whole book, but the story is still emotive. Board book.)

Cooke, T. (2004) *Full, Full, Full of Love*, London: Walker Books. (Jay-Jay's large extended family all have lunch at Grannie's every Sunday. There is always plenty of food to go round and plenty of love.)

Hambelton, L. (2005) *Chameleon Races*, London: Milet Books. (The reptiles have a race, but when they help each other, they have lots more fun. Board book. Available in English and more than ten bilingual editions.)

Mackee, D. (2002) *Elmer's New Friend*, London: Andersen. (All Elmer's old friends are here, but at the very back is a mirror to reflect the child's face so they become Elmer's new friend!)

Melling, D. (2002) *Just Like My Dad*, London: Hodder Children's Books. (A little lion cub wants to grow up to be just like his dad, even though he knows his dad's not perfect and sometimes gets things wrong.)

Shoshan, B. (2006) *Cuddle*, London: Meadowside Children's Books. (A simple rhyming text telling the tale of a little boy who ends up cuddling his teddy because everything else is too big, too tall, too spiky, too dangerous, or too smelly. Board book.)

From 16–36 months

Development matters

- Look to others for responses that confirm, contribute to or challenge their understanding of themselves.

- Can be caring towards each other.

- Learn social skills, and enjoy being with and talking to adults and other children.

- Seek out others to share experiences.

- Respond to the feelings and wishes of others.

Key words

empathy, enjoy company

Main story: *See You Later, Mum!*
(J. Northway (2006), Frances Lincoln, London)

On Monday morning, William went to playschool for the first time, and he was excited, but when he arrived, it was very noisy. He stayed close to Mum, and he was not keen to join in with the activities. He didn't want to paint, so Mum stayed with him. There was another boy who was not very happy either and who stayed near to his mum. On Tuesday, the children were singing songs and clapping. William joined in with the clapping, but he didn't know all the songs. The other boy started clapping, too, when he saw William join in. On Wednesday, William had some playdough, and he offered some to the other boy, but they still wanted their mums to stay. On Thursday, William didn't want to play the jumping-up and falling-down games with the others, but he went over and sat in the big truck with the other boy and found out that his name was David. David said he could drive the truck, but only outside when it wasn't raining. On Friday, the sun was shining, and William couldn't wait to play outside with his new friend in the big truck, and he is at last able to say, 'See you later, Mum!'

This story would be helpful for any child going to playgroup or nursery for the first time. For children who have great difficulty saying 'goodbye' and who cry or cling to their mums, this story can inspire courage and help them not to be afraid. Such a child may need to read the story over and over again before they can finally let their mum leave them. Read the story all the way through the first time and then use it to encourage the children to share their own fears and joys of being in the setting. Especially ask them about their first few days:

- What did they feel like?
- Were they scared about anything?
- Were they excited?
- What helped them to settle in?
- Who tried to help them?
- What did they like to do the best?
- How did they make friends?

Ask the children how they think they can help new children who come to the setting. Adults sometimes take on too much responsibility in this area, whereas there are things that the children could do very well in terms of giving other children a guided tour, inviting them to play, fetching them when it is snack time, and helping them to find their coat when they are ready to explore outside.

Activities

- Continue to spend some individual time playing a game with each of the children that requires passing something back and forth, for example, throwing a ball that they will attempt to catch, chase after and bring back or attempt to throw back, or sending a car backwards and forwards.

- Share books together and respond to their comments. The children will enjoy turning the pages of a book and can be taught to do so carefully. They will point to key characters or lift flaps on the page that they knows conceal a hidden item, or will press a button to make a sound; they will enjoy the 'joke'. Stories about secure loving relationships can help them to talk about the ups and downs of life in the family and with their friends in the setting.

● In a circle time, passing on a pretend hug or a smile can help the children to think about being happy or sad and what they can do if someone is hurt.

Look, listen and note

● Note down how children respond to others within the play situation and generally in the setting. Do they show signs of becoming aware of the need to conform? Are they aware when someone is upset? How do they respond? Do they respond to laughter by joining in and anticipating an amusing situation, in a familiar storybook, for example?

● As the children mature, observe how they approach other children, or groups of children when they want to play. Do they find this easy? What strategies do they employ? Do they initiate role play, inviting others to join them? Do they dominate the play, or are they happier responding to the commands of others?

Effective practice

● Repetition is vital at this stage, and children will have their favourite songs, rhymes and stories that they want over and over again. The key adult needs to be available to provide this stimulation and to share in the fun of these interactions. If you want the children to indicate a choice of song, for example, make sure that a way is found for everyone to communicate their preference. This might mean providing a visual aid that represents a song, for example, a star for 'Twinkle, Twinkle'. This type of support would be particularly useful for children learning English as an additional language, or for those with speech and language difficulties.

- Young children are very sensitive to atmosphere. Body language and the tone of someone's voice 'speaks' in a way that they can understand, even when the words themselves are still unintelligible. The positive relationships that they build up in the home and with the key person in the setting are vital, and a positive environment created in both places does much to enhance the child's confidence in reaching out to others.

- Adult participation in some role-play activities provides opportunities for modelling emotional language. Discussions around their own feelings and the feelings of others support the children in building their relationships with others and in learning how to express their emotions in socially acceptable ways.

- As the children begin to play first alongside, and then with each other, they come up against the need to share, to take a turn in a game or with a toy, to make their own needs known and to respond to the needs of others. They need adult support at this juncture to help them develop these new social skills.

Planning and resourcing

- Practitioners who are regularly evaluating and recording the progress of the children in terms of their relationships with each other must be equally vigilant about reflecting on their own relationships with each other and with the children.

- Regularly check your books and posters for stereotypical images. Check with all members of staff and with a cross-section of parents when buying new reading material, because what may seem acceptable to you might not be to those of a different gender, ethnic group or with a particular disability.

- Use Persona Dolls or choose stories that will challenge the children to think about their relationships with others, particularly those who are different from themselves in some way. Issues can be raised appropriately through story as the children identify with the characters, discuss their actions, reflect on how they might be feeling and think about their dilemmas.

Home links

- Parents and carers should be encouraged to share stories with their children that look at relationships in different contexts. They need to talk to the children about what happens when things go wrong and that they need not be afraid to admit their mistakes. This is true for the adults, too, and is something that can be shared as a joint venture.

- Parents and carers who speak a different first language should be encouraged to share their feelings with their children in their first language and to borrow dual language books from the setting and from the local library. Parents and carers may be willing to translate simple stories onto a tape for use in the library so their own children can continue to develop their first language and other children can enjoy the sounds of another language. If children listen to other languages from a very early age, they are less likely to become afraid of the sounds and think that the people concerned are always talking about them. This is the kind of fear and ignorance that can lead to paranoia and racism.

Additional stories

- Anholt, C. and Anholt, L. (2006) *Here Come the Babies,* London: Walker Books. (Describes what babies are like, what they play with and what they do in a way that their brothers and sisters will enjoy.)

- Braun, S. (2007) *I Love My Daddy,* London: Frances Lincoln. (My daddy wakes me, feeds me, washes me, splashes me, plays with me, chases me, sits with me, yawns with me, tickles me, looks after me, cuddles me.)

- —— (2007) *I Love My Mummy,* London: Frances Lincoln. (In similar vein to the above, but with Mummy as the central character.)

- Cowell, C. (2002) *What Shall We Do with the Boo Hoo Baby?* London: Mantra Lingua. (Cat, Dog, Cow and Duck wonder whether to bathe, feed or play with the baby. This is a story for tired parents and siblings who wonder if the new baby will ever stop crying! Available in English and more than fifteen bilingual editions.)

Garland, S. (1994) *Going to Playschool,* London: The Bodley Head Children's Books. (A multicultural picture book with very simple text showing two children starting at playschool. Their mums stay with them, and they are soon enjoying a game, pouring sand, rolling pastry, painting pictures, dressing up, undressing, having a snack and playing outside – with rabbits!)

Norac, C. (2004) *My Daddy Is a Giant,* London: Mantra Lingua. (A delightful story of a positive relationship between a little boy and his dad, whom he has to climb a ladder to cuddle, but who he knows loves him with all his heart. Available in English and more than twenty bilingual editions.)

Petty, K. (2008) *Ha Ha Baby!* London: Frances Lincoln. (The family gets up to all kinds of antics to try and get their grumpy baby to smile.)

Rock, L. (2004) *Now We Have a Baby,* Oxford: Lion Children's Books. (The middle one of three, a little boy, finds the new baby is noisy and needs a lot of attention, and he feels rather left out. However, he soon discovers that babies need love, too, and that is what helps them to smile and talk and share and care. The focus is on the children's reactions.)

From 30–60+ months

Development matters

- Feel safe and secure, and show a sense of trust.

- Form friendships with other children.

- Demonstrate flexibility and adapt their behaviour to different events, social situations and changes in routine.

- Value and contribute to own well-being and self-control.

Early learning goals

- Form good relationships with adults and peers.

- Work as part of a group or class, taking turns and sharing fairly, understanding that there needs to be agreed values and codes of behaviour for groups of people, including adults and children, to work together harmoniously.

Key words

codes of conduct, friendships

Main story: *Edwardo – The Horriblest Boy in the Whole Wide World*
(J. Burningham (2007), Red Fox, London)

Edwardo was an ordinary boy. Sometimes he would kick things and make a lot of noise. From time to time he was nasty to little children and occasionally he was not very nice to animals. He was not always good at keeping his room tidy and he often forgot to wash his face and brush his teeth.

Read the story right through without stopping. The second time, stop whenever one of Edwardo's characteristics is mentioned and talk to the children about the comment (see below). For example, ask:

- Do you sometimes make a lot of noise?
- Can you think about a time when you did that?
- Why did you do it?
- What did you feel like when you did that?
- What happened?

Further questions:

- Do you think Edwardo was always horrible?
- Was it fair to call him the 'horriblest' in the world?
- How did Edwardo's behaviour change?

- Who helped him to become the loveliest boy in the whole wide world?
- What could we do to help other people?

Activities

- Help the children to create a collage in the setting with photographs and drawings of people and pets that are important to them. This can include family members, but friends and caregivers of all kinds could be included. Use each child's contribution when spending individual time with them to stimulate their talk and share personal experiences with them.

Circle games

- Ask the children to close their eyes for a few minutes and to think of someone special who looks after them. This might be someone inside or outside the family home. Then ask the children what that person does for them, and what makes them special. List the tasks identified by the children and also record the characteristics the children have given that make that person so special to them. Focus on one of the attributes on the list and ask the children to share times when someone cared for them in this way. They can then draw or paint a picture of themselves with this special person, or make a model with playdough or clay. These creations can be added to the collage of those who are important to them.

- Go round the circle and help the children to identify who is sitting next to them and to say, for example: 'I am *Shahid,* and I am sitting next to *Emma.*' It is often soothing for children who are anxious to be able to hold a soft toy when they are speaking. If it is agreed that no one can speak unless they are holding the toy, then this will help with turn-taking, too.

- Go round the circle and ask each child in turn to say something they like about the person next to them. This helps the children to look for the positive attributes of a person, and the child on the receiving end is affirmed. This is particularly helpful if they have a low self-esteem. It makes them feel valued as a member of the group and positive relationships with others seem more possible for them.

- The children could be asked to think of a present they would like to give to the child on their left, for example: 'I will give *Joel* a *football*.' This can be extended to include the reason why: 'because his ball went flat'.

- Ask the children to close their eyes for a few minutes and to think of a friend. Then ask them what they think a friend is, or what they think a friend should be like. Record their answers on a large sheet of paper. When everyone has had time to think and the opportunity to respond, read out one of the characteristics that have been identified on the sheet. Ask the children if they can think of a time when a friend has done this for them. See if anyone would like to share their experience. Other characteristics can be focused on during this session, or later on. Further activities on this theme can include:

- Drawing or painting a picture or making a model with playdough or clay of themselves being a good friend.

- Sharing stories from the list below of lonely people making new friends that can be used to stimulate discussion and to provide ideas for children who find it difficult to relate to others. It can also help children who have lots of friends to consider the feelings of those whom they so often exclude from their games.

- Share the name of a friend. 'My friend is Katie. I can make my friend happy by sharing my farm with her.'

- Talk about how we could make someone feel happier, for example, we could pass on a smile, a hand squeeze or a hug. Practise these around the circle.

- Everyone can stand up and hold hands in a circle and say, 'It's good to have friends' or 'We all like playing and we can all be good friends.' This can be followed up by sending a hand squeeze round the ring.

- Pretend to share something. One of the children goes to the centre of the ring and says, 'I have some grapes to share.' He or she goes round the circle putting an imaginary grape into everyone's hand. The children receive the grape, say thank you and pretend to eat it. Encourage the children to think about the taste and to describe it. Then someone else has a turn. It need not be something to eat, it could be an imaginary toy car, for example, but the children could still describe their cars and pretend to play with them.

- Another time, a real object could be shared. For example, you could give each child a piece of jigsaw so they can complete it together, or some art and craft materials to make a one big collage. Take a photo of the team effort with a caption about working together that can be displayed with the final product.

- Place a hoop on the floor with, for example, six cars, six dolls, six bricks and six balls placed inside. Talk about sharing and how it is important to share with everyone and not just our best friends. Sing the song: 'This is the way we share our toys, share our toys, share our toys, this is the way we share our toys with every one in the nursery' to the tune of 'Here We Go Round the Mulberry Bush'. Ask one child to choose his or her favourite toy from those in the hoop and to give each of the six children an example of the toy, while the others sing the song using the actual toy chosen, 'This is the way we share our bricks ...' Then another child chooses a toy, and the process is repeated.

- Use an action song such as 'Everybody Do This ...'. The children can take turns to devise an action for the others to copy, but they will enjoy having a puppet or a Persona Doll to lead the actions sometimes, too.

- End the session with a simple goodbye song for everyone. For example, 'Goodbye *Katrina*, we're glad you came to play.' Or 'Bye bye, *Amin*, be sure to come again.'

Look, listen and note

- Observe the children's attitude to the collage of people who are important to them. Do they have a wide range of people on the board, or a select few? Do these photographs stimulate their interest? Does their response indicate that they feel safe and cared for by these people? How do they show whether or not this is the case?

- Note whether the child generally finds it easy to relate to adults and to other children, or whether they stand apart and find it difficult to join in.

- When included in a group activity, such as a game, do they understand the concept of rules and turn-taking? Can they wait for their go? Are they able to share?

- Reflect on how the children cope with change, for example, a new member of staff, a change of group within the setting, a new baby at home, moving house.

Effective practice

- Think about each child in the group and of their individual needs and how you can best support them in making positive relationships with the children and adults in the setting. The most enabling environment for some of these activities will be a quiet area, particularly for the more reflective circle games. For each activity, consider how it may need to be adapted to meet the particular needs of that group of children. For example, if you have children going through a silent period while learning English, you will need to think about how the children's first language could be employed, or whether you need more visual supports. If you have children who use wheelchairs or walking frames, then it will be important for all the children to sit on chairs rather than on the floor, as a way of making sure that everyone feels comfortable and included on an equal basis.

- When establishing routines, try to keep these as predictable as possible, as most children will appreciate the security of having certain events that they can rely on every day. For a few children, such routines will be extremely important, and any necessary changes, whether temporary or permanent, should be discussed with them individually if necessary. The children should be consulted about any proposed changes, as far as possible, and the reasons for the changes should be explained and support provided during their instigation. Be ready to spend time listening to the children's opinions and concerns, as well as making your own case.

- Some children will naturally rely on others for help and support, but others will need encouragement to do this. Those who find it easy to form a group should be challenged to find ways of including different people in their play sometimes. Using the Persona Dolls, or through other stories, introduce issues such as making friends. Encourage the children not always to play with the same people. Help them to reflect on what it feels like to be excluded and to think of ways to solve the problem.

Planning and resourcing

- Plan carefully to minimise the amount of change necessary in the core group, keeping the same key people managing the routine events such as transition times at the beginning and end of the session, meal times and rest times. For these events, there needs to be as much stability as possible for the children. During the session, there can be numerous different groupings, both formal and informal, and these should be encouraged particularly where they promote collaborative play and introduce the children to turn-taking and sharing, but the children need to know they have a home base that they can depend upon in times of need, a place where they are well known and where they have established close relationships.

- Keep a large space free for the collage of family and friends, as it could take over a whole wall, and new material will constantly be added. Keep a fresh supply of art materials available nearby with different skin tones in mind, so that the children can include their paintings and drawings of close friends and family members.

- Collect resources for the role-play areas that reflect the cultures of the children in the setting including those with a traveller lifestyle and tradition.

- Involve the children in formulating any regulations or rules for particular activities. The same is as true for the children as it is for the practitioners in that ownership engenders responsibility. We are all far more likely to apply a policy in our practice when we have been involved in the process of composing it and have had the opportunity to consider the issues ourselves.

Home links

- Encourage parents to talk to the children about which photographs they would like to bring to the setting for the collage display. There might be a need for photographs to be specially taken, for example, a child might wish for a neighbour or a friend from across the street to be included.

- Books can also be made of the children participating in nursery activities with a variety of friends, and parents and carers can be asked to contribute photographs from home. Dual-language texts can be added where this is appropriate.

Additional stories

Anholt, L. (2006) *Seven for a Secret,* London: Frances Lincoln. (A poignant tale of a little girl's correspondence with her grandpa until his death leads to a surprise that will change her life for ever.)

Auld, M. (2003) *My Mum,* London: Franklin Watts. (Meet the Family series with six books each about different members of the family.)

Barkow, H. (2006) *Tom and Sofia Start School,* London: Mantra Lingua. (Sofia and Tom have different feelings about their first day at school. Sofia is very excited, whereas Tom is worried in case he gets lost or he won't make any friends. Available in English and more than twenty bilingual editions.)

Beake, L. (2006) *Home Now,* London: Frances Lincoln. (A little girl is orphaned and is helped to have a fresh outlook by an encounter with an orphaned baby elephant. For children aged from five to eight years.)

Binch, C. (2000) *Since Dad Left,* London: Frances Lincoln. (Sid is angry when his parents split up, and he doesn't want to go and stay with his dad for a few days, but by the time he returns home, he feels that he has a dad again. For children aged from five to eight years.)

Child, L. (2008) *You Can Be My Friend,* London: Puffin Books. (Lola is very excited because she is going to spend the afternoon with Morten, the little brother of Charlie's best friend. Useful for discussion on meeting other children for the first time and learning to get along.)

Daly, N. (2007) *Happy Birthday Jamela,* London: Frances Lincoln. (Forced to buy a pair of sensible black shoes that will do for school as well, Jamela decides to brighten them up with glitter and beads. Her mother is very cross, but someone else thinks they look fabulous!)

Gliori, D. (1994) *The Snowchild,* London: Frances Lincoln. (Katie is always left out and doesn't know how to play, but one day when she builds herself a snowchild, she discovers a true friend.)

—— (2005) *No Matter What,* London: Bloomsbury. (A beautifully illustrated and movingly told text of a mother fox's affirmation that she loves her little cub unconditionally, even though Small asks some penetrating questions about the nature of love.)

Green, J. (1999) *Where's My Peg!* Hove: Wayland. (Told in the first person, a little boy relates his first day at school. Sam has been allocated to show him where his peg is, where the toilets are and to make him acquainted with the dressing-up box, the playhouse, the computer, the book corner, the guinea pig and much more. Finally, he paints a picture of his dog, and the teacher writes the dog's name underneath for him to copy. His first day has been such a success that he can hardly wait for the second day.)

Jeffers, O. (2006) *Lost and Found,* London: HarperCollins Children's Books. (A little boy finds a penguin at his door and, believing it to be lost, takes it home to the South Pole, but as he sadly rows away, he sees a dot on the horizon and discovers that the penguin is coming towards him. He was not lost after all, just lonely, and so the two friends are reunited.)

Kemp, J. and Walters, C. (2006) *I Very Really Miss You,* London: Frances Lincoln. (Sam's brother Ben goes away on a school trip, and, at first, Sam is pleased because he can have the bedroom and all the toys to himself, but he soon finds it is too quiet and he misses his brother. What is even more surprising is that his big brother misses him!)

—— (2006) *Time to Say I Love You,* London: Frances Lincoln. (A little girl and her mother have a day out together, and Mum tries to decide the best time to tell her daughter that she loves her.)

Lemmens, R. (2000) *Little Dragon,* London: Mantra Lingua. (Little Dragon is trying to hide from Boy, who frightens him very much, but when they meet, they become firm friends. Available in English and more than five bilingual editions.)

McKimmie, C. (2006) *Brian Banana Duck Sunshine Yellow,* London: Frances Lincoln. (A quirky story of a little boy's search for his own identity and his need to belong.)

—— (2008) *Maisie Moo and Invisible Lucy,* London: Frances Lincoln. (Maisie Moo lives with her parents in the Gone Bonkers Discount Palace. She has an invisible friend called Lucy, with whom she shares all her ups and downs, while she longs for her father to return from his lorry driving.)

Maddern, E. (2007) *Nail Soup,* London: Frances Lincoln. (A traveller is begrudgingly given a bed for the night by a grumpy woman, who says she has nothing for him to eat. He proceeds to make soup from a rusty old nail from his pocket. Plenty of smiles for all.)

Moses, B. (1997) *I'm Lonely,* London: Hodder Wayland. (Useful for talking about loneliness and what can be done about it.)

Northway, J. (2008) *Get Lost, Laura!* London: Frances Lincoln. (Baby Laura keeps getting in the way when her sister and her cousin are playing 'Going to the Ball'. Her sister wishes she would get lost, but when she really does go missing, both the older girls are very anxious.)

Pitcher, C. (2007) *Mariana and the Merchild,* London: Frances Lincoln. (Old Mariana is very lonely and wants a friend, but the village children are afraid of her and the sea-wolves hiding in the caves near her hut. One day, she finds a merbaby in a crab shell and cares for it, although she knows that one day its mother will return to take it home.)

—— (2007) *The Snow Whale,* London: Frances Lincoln. (Laurie and Leo build a snow whale, and it seems to take on a life of its own and inspires their thoughts and dreams.)

Ransome, A. (2007) *Little Daughter of the Snow,* London: Frances Lincoln. (An old Russian couple have no children of their own, so they build a snow girl. She comes alive, but she is not like other children. She plays outside all day and all night, and she eats ice porridge for breakfast.)

Ravishankar, A. (2007) *Elephants Never Forget!* London: Frances Lincoln. (A baby elephant gets lost in the forest and is adopted by a herd of buffalo. He has to decide whether he is now a buffalo or whether he is still an elephant. This story touches on the themes of loss, adoption and integration in a joyful way.)

Ripley, M. (2005) *Private and Confidential,* London: Frances Lincoln. (Laura begins to write to Malcolm in Australia, but when she learns from his sister that he has had an eye operation and is nearly blind, she learns Braille so they can still write to each other.)

Robertson, M. P. (2003) *Big Foot,* London: Frances Lincoln. (A little girl hears a sad song and goes out into the snow to investigate. She gets lost in the snow and encounters a big, hairy creature, but a friendship develops between them.)

Rosen, M. (2003) *lovely Old Roly,* London: Frances Lincoln. (The family dog is very tired and old, and when he dies everyone misses him, but a stray cat comes into their lives and finds a home with them. They don't forget Old Roly and know he will always be with them, but they are glad to be able to care for another pet.

Taylor, K. (2004) *Colletta Goes to School,* Kelsall: Handsome Prints. (The story of a traveller girl starting school.)

Persona Doll story

Introduce the persona over a number of sessions before talking about an issue.

Meet Gavin

Gavin is four years old, and he lives in a village in North Wales with his dad and his older brother, David, who is seven years old. David uses a wheelchair because when he was born his legs wouldn't work, so he can't run and jump like we can. They live in a bungalow, which means there are no stairs. All the rooms are downstairs, even the bedrooms. (*What is your house like? Does it have stairs?*) Dad has put in sliding doors so that David can get in and out of the rooms on his own. There is a button on the wall that Dad and Gavin press to open the doors, but David has a remote control like you use for the television. Gavin would like to have a remote control, too, but Dad says he would have to keep it with him all the time and it might get lost. David has his attached to his wheelchair.

Gavin and David both speak two languages, Welsh and English. (*Can you say 'Hello' in Welsh? Can you say 'Hello' in another language?*) At home, they always speak Welsh. At school, they have some lessons in Welsh and some in English. Because of David's wheelchair, they both get picked up for school in a special minibus. This helps Dad, too, because he doesn't have to worry about getting them to school in the morning. As soon as the minibus has gone, he drives to the factory where he works in the next town. Dad's sister, Auntie Hesper, lives in the next road, and they go to her house when they come home from school. She doesn't live in a bungalow, but David can get through the doors in his wheelchair, and they have a downstairs bathroom. Auntie Hesper has three older children, who go to the big school in the town where Dad works, so they don't get home very early. Gavin loves Auntie Hesper; she always gives them a slice of cake and some juice when they get home from school. 'Just to keep you going until tea time', she always says. Gavin's mum died when he was two. He doesn't remember her very well because he was very small and she was in hospital a lot, but he has lots of photographs of her and David tells him some of the things he remembers.

Dad doesn't usually work on Saturdays unless they have 'a rushed job on'. Gavin doesn't understand what that means, except that Dad doesn't come home until dinnertime and they have to go to Auntie Hesper's for the

Gavin

morning. When Dad is home, they often go into the country. Sometimes David gets sad because he can't climb like Dad and Gavin, but he likes going up Snowdon, which is the highest mountain in Wales, in the little train. There is a special club that takes children climbing in their wheelchairs, and David always gets very excited when he is going on one of those trips. (*Have you ever seen a very high mountain? What would you have to take with you if you were going hillwalking?*) David and Gavin have races sometimes. David races in his wheelchair, and he often wins because he can go very fast and Gavin is still quite little.

Gavin likes school, and he has a special friend called Rees. (*Do you have a special friend? What is he or she like?*) They love to play outside on the bikes, and they have favourite ones that they try to get on first. (*What do you like to play with the most?*) One day they got in trouble because a new boy was riding on Rees's bike, and they told him to get off, and when he wouldn't they pushed him over. (*What do you think the new boy felt like when they did that?*) Mrs Knightley was upset with them. She said she was very disappointed. She talked to them about the new boy and asked them to think about their first day. Gavin could remember his very well. He was scared because he thought they would give him lots of hard sums to do. He remembered crying, too. He had just tipped lots of coloured pegs onto the table ready to put into a big wooden board to make a pattern when he heard a bell ring. He thought it must be playtime, and he couldn't get all those pegs back in the board in time. He didn't know Rees then, and he had felt very lonely. He began to feel sorry for the new boy, and Rees must have, too, because he had his head down. Mrs Knightley asked them what they could do. 'I think we could say sorry', said Gavin, and Rees nodded. 'Good', said Mrs Knightley, 'come over now and meet George properly, because I think two fine boys like you could be my helpers and show him round and sit with him at snack time. Perhaps you could think of a game that you could all play together.' Gavin and Rees felt very proud, and their heads went up. At first, George was frightened of them, but they said they were sorry, and they looked after him all day. They were very glad they had, too, because they found out that George had lots of good ideas of games they could play, and very soon the three of them were always together. They tried to remember, too, that other children could have a turn on the bikes, and they needed to share. (*How can we look after new children? How can we make friends? What does it feel like to be left out, if someone says, 'No, you can't play'?*)

The EYFS principles

The EYFS principles are grouped into four themes which are concerned with the individual needs of the child, the importance of building positive relationships, and the need for the adults in the setting to create an environment that enables the child to learn and to develop to the best of their ability. As these themes relate to this section on making relationships, the focus is on the importance of the children forming effective partnerships with others that enable them to work alongside them companionably. The model set by the staff is very important in this area. It is no use the practitioner expecting the children to include others in their play, to share, to wait for their turn, to be sensitive to the feelings of others, if they consistently ignore a certain child, talk about a member of staff behind their back, or are dismissive of a carer with whom they have close dealings. A team of staff with a strong ethos of care and nurture, and a fierce sense of equality for all, will be in a good position to monitor each other in a supportive and constructive way. Our negative response to a particular child, carer or member of staff might be disguising an underlying prejudice that we are unaware of. We may not even recognise that we are behaving differently towards that person, but if our behaviour has been observed by another member of staff, they have the difficult task of trying to broach the subject with us in a positive way. This is not easy; no one likes to be criticised, and we are all aware that we are far from perfect ourselves, but if the goal is clearly to help everyone to grow in respect and care for each other, then such moments can be liberating for all concerned. Once we have recognised a prejudice within ourselves, then we can begin to deal with it. If the children see that it is possible for the adults in the setting to apologise to each other, to work hard at their relationships, to work collaboratively, to listen actively to each other and to change their behaviour when necessary, then they will feel more comfortable about sharing their worries over their own partnerships. They will come to you confidently knowing that all matters of discrimination will be taken seriously and that they can learn to improve their own relationships and develop the skills necessary to work with and not against others.

4 Behaviour and self-control

From birth–20 months

> ### Development matters
>
> - Are usually soothed by warm and consistent responses from familiar adults.
>
> - Begin to accept care-giving routines.
>
> - Respond to a small number of boundaries, with encouragement and support.
>
> ### Key words
>
> routines, boundaries

Main story: *Busy Baby*
(F. Watt (2005), Usborne Publishing, London, touchy-feely book)

This baby is busy all day: playing with the kitten, reading a book, talking on the phone to friends, riding a tractor, drinking milk and sleeping. During all of these activities, the baby is accompanied by a soft piece of blanket that the children can actually feel. This is a sturdy board book with a simple text that picks out a few key activities that any baby and toddler will be able to relate to. The activities are well chosen to cover all that is needed

CRAVEN COLLEGE

for a healthy lifestyle: nourishment, physical exertion, mental stimulation, communication with others and sleep, all within the comfort zone of the blanket.

Activities

Teething troubles

One of the earliest activities that can necessitate some direction in terms of behaviour is the need for chewing on anything and everything when a child is teething.

- The child needs to be provided with suitable objects, whether commercially produced or household items that they can safely bite on. My daughter adopted a small bottle of hand cream for this purpose. It was almost finished and so was quite flat. It was made of very tough plastic, and the top was tightly screwed on. It was the perfect size for her to grasp, it seemed to be the right shape to give her the maximum comfort, and she could bite on it as hard as she liked with no harmful consequences. I would not have deliberately given her that object, but she discovered it herself and was allowed to use it, as it was not dangerous to her and not precious to me. Other items, however, do not come into this category. For example:

- Chewing paper is very popular with young children and is not to be recommended, but we do want babies to have early access to books. Rag books were the earliest to be developed for babies, and, like the later plastic-leafed books, could be more safely chewed and washed when necessary. Board books can be handled by the babies, but light supervision is needed if they are not to end up with badly chewed corners.

Care of books

In terms of handling books and learning how to treat them, heavy board books provide a halfway house for children to learn to turn pages carefully, but with less opportunity for them to damage the book at a time when their fine motor control is at an early developmental stage. The child needs:

- to learn how to open a book;

- to hold it up the right way to get the maximum understanding from the pictures and the text;

- to look after the books when they are not in use.

The latter is best done by modelling your own careful use of the books and talking about not only their importance but also the pleasure they bring. The message needs to be communicated that books are fun and useful, but at the same time that they are precious and should be treated with respect.

Look, listen and note

Look for the signs that the babies are feeling content and listen for sounds of emerging discomfort. Take careful note of what soothes them and helps them to relax. This will involve discovering their preferred comforter, which may be something brought from home. It could be a particular book, in which case, take note of their treatment of the book.

Effective practice

You need to ensure that there is a smooth transition between the routines of home and those of the setting that will reassure and comfort the babies, but gradually they will need to learn to relate to a wider group of people and to conform to principles of behaviour necessary in the setting, some of which will be different from those of home. The setting boundaries will need to be demonstrated in ways that they will understand and can adhere to. As the babies' development increases so will the expectations of their behaviour, which should be challenging without being unachievable for their stage of development.

Planning and resourcing

Gentle music can be helpful in soothing babies, and lullabies learned from parents and carers will provide a link for the babies between the home and the setting. Those that are in languages other than English can be left on tape to aid practitioners, and the other babies will enjoy listening to the different sounds. At this age, they can still hear and produce many more sounds than will be required in the production of their own first language.

Home links

- If the children are taught respect for their own books, then reading material belonging to the setting and to their parents and carers is more likely to be respected, although pulling books, CDs and videos off shelves presents a very real temptation!

- Practitioners and parents and carers regularly need to share information about teething troubles. This is an uncomfortable time for babies and will almost certainly disrupt sleeping and feeding routines at some point. The children will become fractious and need particular loving support during what is inevitably a very painful time for them. Find out what the parents and carers use to soothe their child and share your own strategies. Other cultures might have their own common practices, and it is as well to know what these are and to be prepared to incorporate new ideas into your own routines.

Additional stories

Allen, J. (2006) *Banana!* London: Frances Lincoln. (A one-word text with a cheeky monkey casting away his banana skins to cause the maximum trouble for the other animals, but in the end the joke backfires on him.)

📖 Batchelor, L. (2001) *Whoops!* Slough: Zero to Ten. (Everyday events using the first single words and phrases that toddlers use: 'yuck', 'all gone', 'hi', 'please', 'thank you', 'bye-bye'.)

📖 Oxenbury, H. (1995) *Playing,* London: Walker Books. (What does a baby play with: blocks, wagon, pot, box, book, Teddy and a ball.)

📖 Pitzer, M. (2004) *I Can, Can You?* Bethesda, Md.: Woodbine House. (Babies and toddlers with Down's syndrome discover that they can draw, find their feet, learn sign language, play by themselves and they ask the reader, 'Can you?')

📖 Watt, F. (2006) *Cuddly Baby,* London: Usborne Publishing. (A baby likes to cuddle floppy rabbit, fluffy pony and a snuggly blanket. Touchy-feely book.)

📖 —— (2006) *Sleepy Baby,* London: Usborne Publishing. (Find out what makes a baby snooze. Touchy-feely book.)

From 16–36 months

Development matters

- Begin to learn that some things are theirs, some things are shared, and some things belong to other people.

- Are aware that some actions can hurt or harm others.

Key words

sharing, cause and effect

Main story: *Be Gentle!*
(V. Miller (2007), Walker Books, London)

This story portrays a common scenario very well. George gives Bartholomew a little kitten to care for with the exhortation that he be gentle with it. But, as with all young children, Bartholomew has to learn to be gentle. At first, it is not within young children's power to be gentle enough, because they are still developing their fine motor skills, but as they develop physically, they still have to learn to be sensitive to the needs of a pet and not to frighten it. So it was with Bartholomew, and he was just too rough with the kitten. He dressed her up, and when he tried to lift her he squeezed too hard. (I wonder how many cats across the whole country have suffered the ignominy of being dressed up and pushed round in prams!) Inevitably, the little kitten had soon had enough and ran away. Bartholomew was distraught and looked everywhere. In the end, he was so upset that he stole away into his secret hiding place under the bed, but to his surprise he found that the little cat was hiding there. The little kitten was, understandably, very anxious at the sight of Bartholomew, but this time Bartholomew put all his effort into being gentle and held the kitten on his lap and stroked her quietly. He was rewarded by hearing her purr very loudly.

This story can lead to discussions with the children about not only their treatment of pets but also the need to be gentle with a new baby brother or sister.

Activities

Besides being gentle, there are other areas of behaviour that are particularly pertinent for children of this age.

Temper tantrums

These can be frightening for young children. Their feelings of frustration take over. They know themselves to be out of control but they do not have the verbal competence to explain themselves, and neither do they have the life experience to know that this feeling will pass and that they are still loved. They are too young to be completely independent but they need to develop a sense of control over themselves and to begin to manage their own actions. Their distress may have any number of causes:

- They might really want to do something but not have the necessary ability. I recently witnessed an eighteen-month-old trying to climb onto a piano stool that was just too high for him. After several determined, but unsuccessful attempts, his frustration levels were visibly growing. Finally, he made one last gargantuan effort and achieved his goal, and we were treated to a Shostakovich-style recital. On this occasion, a major tantrum was averted, but it came very close.

- Children may feel they are being left out in a particular situation, or are being ignored and just want some attention. The arrival of a new baby in the family can potentially be a difficult time for a young sibling, and special thought needs to go into preparing them for the event. Practitioners in a setting have a particular opportunity to give the child some extra attention without the presence of the new baby. There are many stories that tackle this issue, but for toddlers, it will be difficult to discuss the full implications. The most important thing for these children will be the reassurance of a secure, loving relationship affirming that they are still valued and that they still have a place.

- Like any of us, at times children might simply want their own way. When the desired activity is one that is not safe either for the child, or for other children, such as running round the room with a pair of scissors, then the practitioner has no option but to frustrate the child's plans. Sometimes, it is an issue of time. In other words, the activity is appropriate, but something else needs to happen. For example, it might be dinnertime or time to get ready to go home. As part of their social development, children must become accustomed to adapting to the demands of other people's timetabling. Lunch is best eaten when it is still warm, and when a large group of people are involved in a communal activity, there is less flexibility about the time than there might be in a family. However, it is very important to give children a warning when such deadlines are approaching. Respect for the child as a person dictates that they are not suddenly expected to drop everything without any notice, any more than an adult would be expected to.

Dealing with a temper tantrum

- It is important that the adult does not give in as the children need to know where the boundaries lie and that screaming and kicking will not result in their getting their own way. The tantrum should be allowed to burn itself out, as long as the child, or someone else, is not in any danger. The children must learn to recognise, understand and respond to any feeling they have, or that someone else has, but realise that they are not free to behave in any way they like if it causes hurt to another person.

- Sometimes children can be distracted. I remember witnessing a wonderful example of this on holiday in France some years ago. As my family were sitting outside Rouen Cathedral, a group of women and children came meandering along, and the toddler with them suddenly decided that he had had enough; he was not going any farther. So he lay on the pavement and kicked his legs in the air and screamed. No one took much notice for a moment until one of the women came over, looked down at him and shook her head slowly and said what seemed like the equivalent in French of 'Dear, dear!' She then walked a few yards away, bent down and called everyone to look at some little insect she had seen on the pavement. The older children immediately gathered around, and the little boy, seeing that his actions were not having the desired effect, soon got up and toddled off to see what they were all looking at. When they moved off, he happily accompanied them.

The child was not completely ignored, and it is important that even in the middle of a tantrum children know they are cared for. Afterwards, it is appropriate to share a favourite story, to have a snuggling-in time to provide the necessary attention and to reward the controlled behaviour (for strategies that children can develop for themselves, see page 114).

Sharing

As practitioners, we talk a lot about sharing, perhaps too much. The term encompasses a number of different concepts that may confuse young children. We ask them to distinguish between sharing their own toys with a friend who comes to play at home with sharing toys in the setting that belong to everyone and to which everyone has equal rights. In the first context, children give permission for other children to play with their toys for a limited period. In the second situation, there is a social need for some kind of mechanism to make sure that there is fair play for all. In waiting for a turn, children must be able to deal with delayed gratification, and that requires a degree of self-control. In this latter context, taking a turn is the only option and perhaps this term should be used rather than sharing. However, even at home, where giving someone else a turn might not be compulsory, children soon learn that playing with someone else creates more possibilities and is greater fun. Of course, sharing a toy is different from sharing expendable items, which once given can no longer be returned at all, or certainly not in the same form. For example, if children *share* their crisps with a friend, then they are in fact *giving* some of them away. Likewise, if they *share* some of their drawing paper, it may not disappear but it can no longer be used by the original owner; it has become the possession of another child who has made it his or her own by drawing a picture on it. If it were subsequently returned, then it would come as a gift. However, sharing, taking turns and giving to someone else are important aspects of our learned behaviour as we develop social skills. Children can be helped in this by being involved in group activities that require a certain code of behaviour if they are to work successfully. These include activities such as:

- role play

- card games

- guessing games

- circle games

- singing and action rhymes

- playing chase

- playing hide and seek

- ball games

- eating together

- listening to stories

- holding a conversation.

Look, listen and note

Observe children's knowledge of their own belongings and whether they are able to return an item that belongs to someone else. When they are playing, are they able to share the toys with another child, or do they take from other children whenever they want, without regard for the consequences? Are they able to be gentle with any animals in the setting, and around other children? Note any signs of growing frustration and what the causes are. Consider whether these occur in a particular situation or at a particular time of day, or whether there is any other pattern to the behaviour.

Effective practice

Respect children's right to continue with an activity by, for example, taking their snack a little later. Routines are important but need not be totally inflexible, and children need notice, as adults do, if a particular session has to come to an end. This may go some way to alleviating children's frustration and could avert a full-scale temper tantrum. The children also need to know that they can expect to be kept safe from the actions of others, and that they, in their turn, need to be careful not to hurt others by snatching things from them, pushing them out of the way or breaking their toys.

Planning and resourcing

The numbers of popular items in the setting need to be increased to lessen the waiting time for children and to avoid a build-up of unnecessary frustration. The children can be given some responsibility for the ordering of materials. Pictures of items from catalogues can be displayed for children to indicate their preferences by putting a star under the picture, for example. Clear procedures need to be established so that all the stakeholders in the setting understand why and how events are managed and have ownership of the policies and practices of the setting. This exchange may include using an interpreter, either formally or informally, depending on the situation, for children who are learning English as an additional language. These lists of procedures need to include, for example, some simple strategies worked out with the children for helping them to deal with their behaviour when their feelings are threatening to overwhelm them or have already spiralled out of control.

Home links

- Exchange information with parents and carers about preparing children for the arrival of a new baby. This is obviously more difficult when the children are under two and cannot fully understand what is happening. Encourage parents to be especially careful to show their continuing affection and to plan for time alone with the children, which is not easy with the, often unpredictable, demands of a new baby. But again, a few minutes peace snuggled up on the sofa sharing a book can provide a breather for the parent and be an affirmation for children that they are still loved and have not been replaced. It is important not to place too much emphasis on the fact that children will be able to play with their new brother or sister, as this is often the biggest disappointment in the first few months. Talk about being gentle will be very pertinent, too, at this time. If the children have already learned how to treat their pets, then this will be helpful when they are interacting with the new baby.

- Life at home is where young children will first learn to make relationships and to learn what fitting in with the family means. Older brothers and sisters may be loving and tolerant to a certain extent but will not be happy with little fingers chewing and dribbling over their prized possessions, and young children gradually learn that some things belong to them but that other things are the property of other members of the family.

- It is at home, initially, that children learn their social skills, and it is in this area that tensions can arise between the home and the setting. There can be differences in expectations within any family, but for those from a different cultural background, the problems may be exacerbated. For example, in the United Kingdom, the social-communication wheels are oiled by the persistent use of 'please' and ' thank you'. Children must learn this for their social survival, but practitioners must be aware that in other languages there are different ways of signifying politeness. The subtleness of this can often be lost in translation, and parents and carers may appear rude in their interactions with practitioners. Indeed, they may find it offensive that the same words are used after you have received the milk jug from someone as you would use when you say, 'Thank you for saving my life.' This whole area will need to be explored sensitively with parents and carers for the mutual benefit of all concerned.

Additional stories

Donaldson, J. (2007) *Sharing a Shell,* London: Campbell Publishers. (A little hermit crab learns the benefits of being willing to share his shell with a purple anemone and a tickly bristleworm.)

Grindley, S. and Ellis, A. (2000) *Can We Play Too, Piglittle?* London: Orchard Books. (Piglittle won't share his ball with his friends but soon discovers it's no fun playing on his own.)

Hamilton, R. (2007) *Let's Take Over the Nursery,* London: Bloomsbury Publishing. (When the teacher is trapped in the climbing frame, the toddlers run riot. They paint everything and push the cooker down the slide, but when one child begins to cry and then another, it becomes imperative that Miss Tuck is rescued.)

Jadoul, E. (2006) *Just a Little Bit.* Slough: Zero to Ten. (Olive has a long scarf to keep out the cold. Bird comes along and wants to share, and then Rabbit, but when Fox arrives, the others really have doubts about whether there is anything left to share. Fox walks sadly away, but Olive relents and says she is sure that they can find just a little bit more. Board book.)

Latimer, M. (2008) *Emily's Tiger,* Bath: Barefoot Books. (Whenever Emily doesn't get her own way, she roars like a tiger, until Grandma comes to stay. This story shows children how to manage their feelings of frustration and anger.)

Llewellyn, C. (2001) *Why Should I Share?* London: Hodder Wayland. (Told in the first person by a little boy who is in trouble with his mum and who has upset his brother and lost his friends all because he won't share, but his best friends next door are twins and tell him that everything is much more fun if you share. The little boy is won round and when he begins to share his things, he finds that other people begin to share their things with him.)

Ormerod, J. (2005) *When an Elephant Comes to School,* London: Frances Lincoln. (This covers a first day at nursery in great detail, but through the focus of a baby elephant. It is amusing and children who are a little nervous about starting school should find this reassuring.)

Ross, T. (2006) *Say Please,* London: Andersen Press. (The Little Princess learns that by saying 'please' and 'thank you' she gets on better than when she screams and shouts.)

Teckentrup, B. (2008) *Grumpy Cat,* London: Frances Lincoln. (Grumpy Cat likes to be alone, but a little kitten wants to be with him, follows him around and keeps wanting to snuggle up. Grumpy tries all sorts of ways to get rid of the kitten but without much success. However, when the kitten finally disappears, Grumpy Cat realises that he feels rather lonely.)

Vipont, E. (1971) *The Elephant and the Bad Baby,* London: Puffin Books. The elephant carries the baby all over town, and he takes ice creams, pies, buns, crisps, biscuits, lollipops and apples and never once says 'please'. The shopkeepers are in hot pursuit, but all ends happily when the baby learns to say 'please', and his mother makes pancakes for everyone.)

Wilson, J. (2000) *Jimmy Jelly,* London: Frances Lincoln. (Little Angela is mad about a television personality called Jimmy Jelly. The rest of the family cannot stand him, until he comes to open a shop in their town.)

From 30–60+ months

Development matters

- Begin to accept the needs of others, with support.

- Show care and concern for others, for living things and the environment.

- Show confidence and the ability to stand up for own rights.

- Have an awareness of the boundaries set and of behavioural expectations in the setting.

Early learning goals

- Understand what is right, what is wrong, and why.

- Consider the consequences of their words and actions for themselves and others.

Key words

moral judgements, consequences

Main story: *When Sophie Gets Angry – Really, Really Angry*

(M. G. Bang, (2008), Scholastic Children's Books, London)

Sophie has a falling-out with her sister because she doesn't want to share. Her mother takes her sister's side, and then Sophie falls over a truck and hurts herself. That is the last straw, and she roars a red, red roar, and she runs and runs and runs until she cannot run anymore, and then she has a good cry. At that point, she begins to come out of her rage. Sophie has a special place that she retreats to in times of stress. It is an old beech tree that she climbs into overlooking the seashore near to her house where she has found comfort before. It is important to stress with the children that although Sophie ran and ran, she did not run away. Physical exertion is one way of getting rid of pent-up energy and crying, too, can be an emotional release. Children will need to find strategies for dealing with their anger, and it is often easier to talk about a situation through a story. The focus here is on

Sophie's anger, so children can contribute to the analysis of the situation and talk about their own feelings without making them the centre of attention. Talk about the need everyone has for places to go where they can be quiet, think, and not be disturbed. Children will need to discover such places that they can visit at any time, but especially at times of tension and distress. In this story, by the time Sophie returns home, she is feeling better. Home is described as warm and smelling good, and everyone is pleased to see her.

Activities

Controlling anger

Here are some simple strategies that children can develop to enable them to take control of their own behaviour when they feel anger or frustration arising:

- Take three or four deep breaths. (They will need to be taught how to do this.)

- Count slowly to five.

- Press the pause button to give themselves time to think things through and decide what to do.

- Find a quiet place, perhaps some special place where they like to go anyway.

- Get involved in some physical activity, such as cycling round the garden on one of the bikes as fast as they can.

Resolving conflict

Children can be involved in the discussion of sensitive issues around social and emotional development. Very young children recognise difference, and, by the age of three, they begin to make judgements based on the messages they have absorbed from their environment and to act accordingly. For example, if they have learned that it is better to be a girl than a boy, or better to have a lighter skin than a darker one, then they need to be challenged about these things, albeit appropriately for their age and their experience, and story is the most natural way to do this. If an issue has arisen in the setting that needs examining further, this can be tackled through:

- reading one of the stories given here and following up with a discussion based round the actions of the characters;

- telling a Persona Doll story to introduce the issue you wish to discuss;

- creating a play using puppets.

If it is the puppet that has misbehaved, or that has got into trouble through no fault of their own, then all the children can join in offering solutions, in the same way they do with the story character or with a Persona Doll. Sometimes practitioners take it on themselves to act out a scenario, and this can have a powerful effect on the children.

If the children are involved in empathising and solving problems, they can begin to take control of their own conflicts and bring about their own resolutions. At this point, the practitioner needs to hold back for longer to allow this to happen and only step in on safety grounds. However, there is another major area that needs attention before the children are able to take over this amount of control, and that is to provide them with a strong foundation in emotional literacy. They will need to be able to name a feeling that they have recognised if they are to communicate and reflect with other children on their own actions and those of others. This language will need to be modelled, initially, by the practitioners and the children encouraged, and given the opportunity, to use their newly acquired vocabulary. This can be achieved through activities such as the games that focus on feelings (see p. 63), and through discussions during storytelling sessions. As their vocabulary grows, the children's ability to moderate their behaviour will develop. Behaviour that is named and reflected on will not seem so overwhelming and frightening.

Look, listen and note

Observe the children's development in terms of how they relate to others. Do they notice when someone is hurt? Do they recognise the consequences of their own actions? Are they taking any responsibility for those actions? Note their behaviour in conflict situations. Can they remain calm and find a solution? Listen to their use of emotional vocabulary and note any additions. If they have a violent outburst, can they put into place any of the strategies that have been discussed?

Effective practice

Be effective in your demonstration of concern for other people and for all living things. Discuss care of pets, both those in the setting and those at home. Let the children see that you behave consistently to everyone and that you are firm and fair. Increasingly, give the children the opportunity to resolve their own conflicts. Discuss why boundaries are necessary and help them to understand why it is wrong to take other people's things and why shouting at someone or pushing them out of the way upsets them. Talk to them about how another person might be feeling. Be ready to admit your mistakes and show the children that we all get things wrong sometimes and we need to say we are sorry.

Planning and resourcing

Involve the children in setting the rules for care of their environment. Explain why limits have to be set so that everyone can be safe. Provide stories dealing with topics that are of current concern to the children so that everyone can contribute to the discussion. Listen to the children's views on events they consider to be unfair and help them to learn to understand the behaviour of others through empathising with the characters in the stories.

Home links

Discussion with parents and carers on discipline and all matters of acceptable behaviour needs sensitive handling. The expectation of behaviour in the home and in the setting might be diverse, and an understanding needs to be established that everyone is comfortable with. Also, children's behaviour might differ dramatically according to the environment. For example, their behaviour may be reported as being very difficult to manage at home, and yet those same children can be very quiet and amenable in the setting, or vice versa. Those in the setting involved in the care and nurture of the children need to keep both sets of behaviours in mind when drawing up their profile and planning for their learning and development. As always, the more trusting and non-judgemental the relationship is between the practitioners and the parents and carers, the easier it will be to share information and to work together for the benefit of the child.

Additional stories

Argent, K. (2006) *India the Showstopper,* London: Frances Lincoln. (When India, the elephant, behaves badly, she loses her place in the limelight. It is then that she discovers the true value of friends.)

Barkow, H. (2005) *Little Red Hen and the Grains of Wheat,* London: Mantra Lingua. (Retelling of the classic tale of the hen who sows her wheat, waters it, harvests it, grinds it into flour and makes a loaf of bread. She does this all alone because her friends refuse to help her, although, of course, everyone is keen to eat the bread. Available in English and thirty bilingual editions.)

Baumgart, K. (2003) *Laura's Secret,* London: Little Tiger Press. (Laura and her little brother Tommy make a kite and take it to the park, but it does not fly very well, and they are teased by some older boys. This is taken further when Tommy is alone and the same boys bully him, but Laura uses her special star to weave some magic and boost their confidence.)

Boyd, S. (2006) *Calm Down, Boris!* London: Templar Publishing. (Boris is an orange hairy monster who means well but is rather too enthusiastic in his responses. Invites to brush his hair and to feed him result in being smothered with kisses. He is too loud and boisterous for the other little monsters in the park but when a big dog jumps over the fence, Boris is the hero as he chases the dog away with big friendly kisses.)

Child, L. (2000) *I Want a Pet!* London: Frances Lincoln. (Written in the first person, a little girl tries to find a pet that no one in the family will object to: Grandad says sheep follow you around, Dad says wolves give him a headache, and Mum is not in favour of having bats in the wardrobe!)

Child, L. (2006) *But Excuse Me That Is My Book,* London: Puffin Books. (On a visit to the library, Lola is dismayed when her best book in the whole world, *Beetles, Bugs, and Butterflies* is taken out by someone else. Charlie solves the matter by getting her interested in *Chimps and Chimpanzees*; now that is her best book ever.)

—— (2007) *Whoops! But It Wasn't Me,* London: Puffin Books. (Charlie brings a rocket home that he has made at school. He is very proud of it; it is the best thing he has ever made. He warns Lola not to touch it, but she cannot resist. It takes her quite a while before she can own up.)

Daly, N. (2008) *Pretty Salma,* London: Frances Lincoln. (This is a modern 'Red Riding Hood' story set in a South African township. It features Anansi as the storyteller and the sly, no-good Mr Dog.)

Genechten, G. V. (2004) *Floppy's Friends,* London: Mantra Lingua. (Floppy's friends will only play with their own special friends and not with the other rabbits. One day, a new rabbit arrives, and they make fun of him because he doesn't know their game, but it turns out that the new rabbit has a really good new game to contribute. Available in English and more than twenty bilingual editions.)

Gliori, D. (2008) *Little Bear and the Wish Fish,* London: Frances Lincoln. (The bears of the Papana River Valley have everything they need but they are always complaining. One day the Raindancer, the Sunblazer and the Snowmaker decide to send a wish fish to teach them a lesson.)

Hayes, S. (2004) *Mary, Mary,* London: Walker Books. (Mary is contrary, and when everyone else is afraid of the giant, she goes right up to his house. She finds he is sad, not wicked, and she soon sorts him out and turns his garden into a playground for the children.)

Hobbs, L. (2004) *Horrible Harriet,* London: Frances Lincoln. (Horrible Harriet lives in a nest in the roof of the school, and all the children are scared of her, but one day Athol the Egghead lands in a hot-air balloon and Harriet makes her first friend.)

—— (2005) *Hooray for Horrible Harriet,* London: Frances Lincoln. (Mr Chicken terrorises the whole school, but Harriet is his friend and she can handle him and so becomes popular with the children for a short time at least.)

Jenkin-Pearce, S. (1997) *Annie Angel,* London: Frances Lincoln. (Annie has always wanted to be an angel, and on her birthday she receives a beautiful pair of wings from her grandma, but she soon discovers that being angelic is not so easy.)

Koralek, J. (2004) *The Coat of Many Colours,* London: Frances Lincoln. (The Bible story of Joseph whose father gave him a coat of many colours because he was his favourite son. His brothers were jealous and decided to teach him a lesson.)

Lurie, A. (2007) *Baba Yaga and the Stolen Baby,* London: Frances Lincoln. (Elena should be minding her baby brother as the black geese have been flying over the village stealing children for the witch Baba Yaga, but instead she runs off to play with her friends and leaves the baby alone. A Russian folktale.)

Maddern, E. (1996) *Rainbow Bird,* London: Frances Lincoln. (The traditional Aboriginal fire myth retold. Bird Woman manages to outwit Crocodile Man who had put himself in charge of Fire and kept the rest of the world cold and dark.)

Monks, L. (2007) *No More Eee-orrhh!* London: Egmont Press. (Dicky Donkey is driving everyone crazy with his constant eee-orrhhing, but then he suddenly loses his voice and has to go to the animal hospital. His neighbours realise that they miss his early morning call and are pleased when he gets his voice back and is ready to leave the hospital, which is not a moment too soon for the hospital staff!)

Moodie, F. (2007) *Noko's Surprise Party*, London: Frances Lincoln. (Takadu the aardvark invites all the animals to Noko's surprise birthday party except for the greedy hyena, who does his best to spoil the party by stealing the figs that Takadu has spent all day picking.)

Moses, B. (1994) *I Feel Jealous*, London: Hodder Wayland. (Lots of descriptions of what it is like to feel jealous as experienced by young children, for example, like a green-eyed monster all twisted up inside. Various solutions are offered.)

—— (1998) *I Don't Care*, London: Hodder Wayland. (This is about respect and what that means. It includes respect for animals and places and for yourself.)

—— (1998) *It's Not Fair*, London: Hodder Wayland. (To feel hard done by is to be like a bee that can't reach a flower, or a big cat trapped behind bars, or …)

—— (1998) *It Wasn't Me*, London: Hodder Wayland. (This is about honesty and includes a focus on topics such as accidents, blame, forgiveness, owning up and telling white lies.)

Northway, J. (2008) *Lucy's Quarrel*, London: Frances Lincoln. (Lucy and her cousin Alice are best friends but in the lead-up to Lucy's birthday party, Alice says she is bossy and they have a big quarrel.)

Olten, M. (2008) *Boys Are Best!* London: Frances Lincoln. (Two boys who think that boys are best and that girls are pointless and silly find their views challenged when the subject of ghosts is brought up.)

Onyefulu, O. (2007) *Chinye*, London: Frances Lincoln. (A West African story of goodness and greed and how the life of a little girl called Chinye is transformed by the magic of the gourds.)

Patten, H. (2000) *Clever Anansi and Boastful Bullfrog*, London: Frances Lincoln. (Bredda Croaky is a special bullfrog whose skin glistens with beautiful colours but he croaks all day long. In desperation, Anansi the spider decides he must take action to silence Bredda. A Caribbean tale.)

Peters, A. F. and Peters, P. (2008) *The No-No Bird*, London: Frances Lincoln. (No-No Bird's favourite word is 'No!' He refuses to play with Little Mouse or climb trees with Squirrel, but when he meets Snake and discovers that No-No Bird is his favourite food, he quickly changes his tune!)

Pitcher, C. (2005) *Nico's Octopus,* London: Frances Lincoln. (A little boy called Nico rescues an octopus caught in a fisherman's net and keeps it as a pet. He finds it can do some amazing things like pulling a cork from a bottle, but after a while it becomes ill and Nico knows he must let it go back into the sea. For children aged from five to eight years.)

Roddie, S. (2007) *Best of Friends,* London: Frances Lincoln. (Even best friends need some privacy, so the friendship between Hippo and Pig is sorely tested when Hippo cuts down the hedge between their two houses.)

Rosen, M. (2007) *Songbird Story,* London: Frances Lincoln. (Two songbirds are separated when caught by the birdcatcher. The story tells how they are eventually reunited and find their freedom.)

Ross, T. (2007) *I Want a Cat,* London: Andersen Press. (Jessy feels very hard done by because every one else has a pet and she does not, and she would really like a little cat.)

Scott, N. K. (2006) *Mangoes and Bananas,* London: Frances Lincoln. (Kanchil the mouse deer and Monyet the monkey plant some fruit trees together, but when the fruit is ripe, Monyet cannot resist eating it all, and Kanchil cannot help getting even.)

Simon, F. (2008) *Don't be Horrid, Henry!* London: Orion Children's Books. (Horrid Henry tries his best to get rid of his new baby brother, Perfect Peter, but to no avail. As Peter gets bigger, Henry gets more and more angry, until one day he saves Peter from a fierce dog and decides that he rather likes being a hero.)

Souhami, J. (2006) *The Leopard's Drum,* London: Frances Lincoln. (Osebo the leopard has a beautiful drum but he will not let anyone else play it, not even Nyame the sky-god. Nyame offers a big reward to anyone who can bring him the drum. Plenty of animals try but in the end it is a very small tortoise who succeeds.)

Thomas, P. (2007) *I'm Telling the Truth,* London: Hodder Wayland. (Talking about honesty in an accessible way for young children.)

—— (2000) *Stop Picking On Me,* London: Hodder Wayland. (Introduces talk about the causes and effects of physical and verbal bullying and encourages children to talk to someone who can do something about it.)

Willis, J. and Ross, T. (2006) *The Really Rude Rhino,* London: Andersen Press. (Little Rhino is rude to every one, sticking out his tongue, making rude noises and waving his bottom at them, until at last he meets his match in the form of a little girl who is eating water melon.)

Wilson, B. K. (2004) *Maui and the Big Fish,* London: Frances Lincoln. (This is a Polynesian tale of baby Maui who was carried away by the god Tama to learn magic. When he returns, his brothers make fun of him and will not take him fishing with them, but he soon outwits them.)

Persona Doll story

Introduce the Persona Doll over a number of sessions before talking about an issue.

Meet Rajia

Rajia (pronounced Razia) is four years old. She lives with her mummy and daddy and her grandparents. She calls her grandma 'Nani' and her grandpa 'Nana' because they were born in Bangladesh. They came to England when Rajia's mummy was five years old. Her daddy came to England when he married her mummy, and he works in his uncle's restaurant. Rajia's mummy works in a care home for elderly people. She enjoys her work but sometimes she feels sad because some of the people have no one to visit them. Some of the careworkers stay all night, but Rajia's mummy only does the day shift, although it makes it difficult for her to see daddy sometimes because he goes to work at about four o'clock in the afternoon and gets back very late at night after the restaurant has closed. Nani does most of the cooking, and she is nearly always at home, which makes Rajia feel safe.

Rajia

Rajia's family live in two terraced houses which are joined together, but they do not have to go out of one front door and into the next one, because they have a door inside between the two houses. They have two houses because they have a large family. (*Where do you live? What sort of house do you live in?*) Rajia has a big brother called Mohammad Aziz, who is eight years old; another brother, Mohammad Badrul, who is six years old; a sister, Aisha, who is three years old; and a baby brother who is eighteen months old, who is called Mohammad Shakil, and he sleeps in Mummy and Daddy's room. Rajia and Aisha share a bedroom, and they sleep in bunk

123

beds. Rajia sleeps on the top, because Aisha is only three, and Mummy thinks she might fall out. Rajia is very careful when she climbs the ladder up to her bed. (*Have you got any brothers and sisters? Where do you sleep? Do you share a bedroom? Do you like sharing/having your own room? Why?*)

Rajia has just started school, and Aisha has started at the nursery. Nana takes the girls to school every day. Rajia is very fond of him and usually tells him if anything is worrying her. (*Who takes you to school every day?*) Rajia does not really like to sit still for very long. She likes to play in the sand and the water, although she will sit still to listen to stories, and, in fact, she is very good at making up stories herself. She has lots of friends because she can always think of good games to play at break time, and after school she goes with Aisha to play on a patch of rough ground opposite to where they live. (*Tell us about your favourite game? Do you have a special friend to play with? What is he or she like? Where do you play?*)

There are no pets in the house, but Rajia would really like to have a little cat. She keeps asking, but no one has said she can yet. There is a dog called Rusper who lives in her road, and she talks to him when she goes past, although he makes her jump sometimes when he barks suddenly. (*Do you have a pet? How do you look after it? If you could choose a pet, what would you like?*)

Rajia's favourite food is dhal sauce and rice, which her Nani cooks. She likes to eat chips too and goes with her big brothers to the fish and chip shop. She is fond of crisps, although she is not allowed to have them very often. She says that some of her friends cannot say 'crisps' very well and call them 'crips', but Rajia can speak English and another language called Sylheti Bengali really well. (*What do you like to eat? What's your favourite food?*)

Rajia's brothers go to the mosque every day after school, and they learn to read and write in a language called Urdu and to read the Qur'an, their special book, in another language called Arabic. Sometimes Rajia watches Bollywood films with the rest of the family, and they speak in a language called Hindi; she understands a lot of the words, especially with the pictures to help her. Aisha can speak Sylheti Bengali and understands a lot of English, but she hasn't spoken to anyone at nursery yet. She knows that none of the teachers can speak Sylheti, and she feels too shy to speak in English in case she makes a mistake. Her teacher is not worried, and she has told Nana that Aisha seems happy and joins in all the activities with the other children and they keep talking to her and including her in all the games. Nana was not worried, he knows that Aisha will speak when she is ready, and he gave her a big hug. (*What languages can you speak? Have you heard someone speaking a different language? Have you listened to the stories in the listening corner? Some of them are told in a different language.*)

One day, something happened that made Rajia and Aisha feel very sad. It happened on a Saturday morning. Rajia and Aisha were sitting on their front doorstep, and they were very excited because on the piece of rough ground across the road, some workmen had come and had started to build a new playground. Rajia and Aisha were watching the men carefully, and Rajia was telling Aisha some of the games they could play. Aisha was looking forward to having a go on the swings, but Rajia knew there was going to be a ladder up to a house with a rope bridge going across to a climbing frame in the shape of a space rocket, because she had seen the pictures at school. (*What would you like in a new playground?*) Rajia was just telling Aisha about these pictures, when a big girl came and stood in front of them. Rajia had seen her before because she took her little brother to Aisha's nursery. She leaned over and pointed to Aisha and said to Rajia, 'Is that your sister? My brother says she can't talk, she must be really stupid.' And she ran off down the road shouting, 'Stupid, stupid!' (*What do you think they felt like, when she said that?*) Rajia and Aisha were very upset. Aisha started to cry because the girl spoke very loudly and frightened her. Rajia went very quiet, and she had a funny feeling in her tummy, but she was cross as well. She didn't know what to do, and she hasn't told anybody about it. She thought she would come and tell you and see if you could help her decide what to do. (*What do you think Rajia should do? Can you help her?*)

 The EYFS principles

The EYFS principles are grouped into four themes that are concerned with the individual needs of the child, the importance of building positive relationships, and the need for the adults in the setting to create an environment that enables the child to learn and to develop to the best of their ability. As these themes relate to this section on behaviour and self-control, they are specifically about helping each child to learn and to develop a growing understanding of what is right and wrong, and why. Through sharing these stories and activities, children have the opportunity to distance themselves from a particular situation, to reflect on how the characters in the story might be feeling, and how the actions of other people have contributed to that. Development in this area will involve the children learning to control their own behaviour, so that they will feel in control of themselves and others will feel safe around them. It will also involve them in curbing their own determination to be first at any cost and to grab the best of whatever is on offer. Through control of their behaviour, they will be helped to establish right relationships with people. They will discover that those who will not share with others soon find themselves lonely, as no one else will want to share with them. They will need to reflect too on the impact their words and actions will have on others. To call someone names because they are different from you may seem a small thing, but children need to understand that it can hurt the other person for a very long time, and make them feel sad, and that to tell someone they cannot play with you is unkind.

It is the responsibility of the adults in the setting to ensure that the children are supported in learning these life lessons and are helped to develop strategies for coping with difficult situations, whether it be that their frustration has boiled over into a temper tantrum, or they have fallen out with their best friend, excluded someone from a game, or feel upset because they do not know how to help someone who is in trouble. Learning to behave in a socially acceptable manner that remains creative requires an environment where controlled behaviour is demonstrated, where the adults offer support and encouragement and challenge to the children, but who are not afraid to admit that they, too, make mistakes and that we can all help each other to get things right next time!

Self-care

From birth–20 months

Development matters

- Anticipate food routines with interest.
- Express discomfort, hunger or thirst.
- Begin to indicate own needs, for example, pointing.
- May like to use a comfort object.

Key words

physical needs, comfort

Main story: *Peepo!*
(A. Ahlberg (1997), Puffin Books, London, board book)

The book follows a baby through a whole day and begins with the scene of him in his cot. Each page has a peephole to prompt anticipation of what is coming next. This includes the hustle and bustle of the kitchen from his highchair and activities in such places as the living room, the backyard and the park. The first page begins with the rhyme, 'Here's a little baby, one, two, three. Stand in his cot, what does he see?' and the answer is also written in rhyme. On this page, the baby looks through the hole and sees his parents in their big brass bed. This pattern is repeated until the very last page, which ends with, 'Here's a little baby, one, two, three. Fast asleep and dreaming, what did he see?' This will stimulate an immediate recall of all the baby has seen throughout the day. The setting is quaint, with Mum wearing a hairnet in bed, coal being brought in for the fire, a range in the kitchen (now popular again!) and old-fashioned toys, but the detail is such that there is so much to talk about at many different levels. Very young children will simply enjoy the peek-a-boo factor; older children will be able to identify and reflect on an environment that is both similar and different from their own. Some adults have been haunted by the hidden depths of the question, 'What does he see?' One reviewer wrote, 'Its hints of a darker world-drama beyond the crib never once overshadow the brilliant beauty and innocence of this book, at least for the very young children it will be read to.'

Activities

Babies at this stage are still very much concerned with the basic human needs of food, sleep, warmth and comfort. Bottle-feeding in the setting keeps babies close to a supportive adult to whom they look to provide all their needs and with whom communication is paramount whether it be to signal their need for milk, a clean nappy, a reassuring voice or a nap. Self-care at this stage is unconscious, more of a primal instinct, but gradually, as babies develop, they begin to take an interest in the routines that nourish and sustain them. The signalling becomes more and more refined, the crying increasingly gives way to pointing and to verbal clues. Remember to talk to babies about the routines of the day so that the sounds of the words become familiar to them. As you speak, hold up the object you are referring to, so babies can begin to associate the two. For example, as you get ready to change babies' nappies:

- Name the items: 'Here's your changing mat, let's put it over here. Now where's your clean nappy? Oh, here it is. Can you see the wipes? Oh, they're on the shelf. I will just get some warm water in a little bowl and a cloth to dry your bottom. Now let's have a look. Let's get this wet nappy off. Oh, that's better isn't it? You can have a good kick. We'll soon have you feeling clean and dry again ...'

- Make up little repetitive jingles to accompany each stage of the process. 'Here's your mat, mat, mat. How about that, that, that.' Don't worry about what anyone else thinks, this is a one-to-one time for you and the baby to communicate with each other and for them to learn about routines within the setting and start to anticipate what comes next while enjoying the full attention of a supportive adult.

- An older child might be holding a toy, and you can sing an appropriate song. For example, for a bus, you could sing, 'The Wheels on the Bus Go Round and Round', or for a doll, 'Miss Polly Had a Dolly.'

Look, listen and note

Patterns will emerge in terms of the babies' need for food and they will begin to respond to food in different ways. Keep a note of their reactions to the prospect of food and to different foods as they are weaned. Be particularly aware of any adverse physical reactions to a particular food that might indicate an allergy. Record any significant developments in their means of communication. These will result not only around food but when they wish to signal a nappy change or that they are tired or want their comforter.

Effective practice

Encourage babies to increasingly participate in their feeding and drinking. Remember that eating with their hands, although very messy, will increase their opportunities for sensory awareness. All kinds of beakers with tops are available now to help them drink independently from a very young age, when their fine motor control is not sufficiently developed for them to drink from an ordinary cup.

Planning and resourcing

Plan feeding times as far as possible to dovetail with home routines, and, as the child is weaned, find out about cultural and religious preferences and restrictions with regard to food. Children from observant Muslim or Jewish households, for example, will not eat meat from pigs in any form, or other meat that has not been killed in a particular manner with the appropriate prayers being said. Neither will they eat anything containing animal fat, which has far wider consequences, and products need to be constantly checked, particularly jellies and foods made with gelatine. Fortunately, vegetable-based oils and fats are now far more prevalent than they once were.

Home links

Practitioners need to familiarise themselves with the routines established at home around feeding and sleep patterns and see how these can be aligned to those of the setting, particularly in the early days. For example:

- If the baby is being breastfed at home, then breast milk can be expressed for use in the setting during the day if the baby is in day care. Families will differ, too, in their preferences for introducing their child to solid food, and this needs to be discussed thoroughly with the parents and carers. Provide utensils that encourage babies to gradually take over more control of their own feeding.

- Some families prefer their children to have a regular time for sleeping, and others like them to sleep whenever they feel like it. For some, sleeping is a communal activity, for example, snuggling up with parents and siblings, while others prepare for sleep time by singing lullabies and rocking the child. It will be helpful for the child to have something from home to be a comfort to them, a connection with home during their sleep time.

- If the parents and carers speak languages other than English, then care must be taken to enable them to explain how their children communicate their needs. Other adults from the community might be able to help with this informally if you have no bilingual staff who share those particular languages.

Additional stories

Anholt, L. (2007) *Chimp and Zee's Clothes,* London: Frances Lincoln. (Chimp and Zee dress up in a variety of clothes. A colourful book with a simple text for babies and toddlers. Board book.)

Bradman, T. (2008) *Daddy's Lullaby,* London: Bloomsbury. (Dad comes home very late and finds only the baby awake. They go on a journey round the house together looking at the cat, the baby's brother and mum sleeping, and finally they both fall asleep on the sofa, and that is where the rest of the family find them in the morning. Board book.)

Dorling Kindersley (2004) *My First Body Board Book,* London: Dorling Kindersley. (A word and picture book of the parts of a baby's body and their uses.)

Hayes, S. (2007) *Eat up Gemma,* London: Walker Books. (Gemma refuses to eat, throws her breakfast on the floor, squashes grapes, feeds her dinner to the dog, until sitting in church one day, her brother has an idea.)

Hollyer, B. (2001) *The Bloomsbury Book of Lullabies,* London: Bloomsbury. (Beautiful book of rhymes to share before bed.)

Inkpen, M. (2007) *Wibbly Pig's Silly Big Bear,* London: Hodder Children's Books. (Wibbly Pig's new friend doesn't know how to brush his teeth, comb his hair or use a spoon, but Big Bear is loved just the same.)

McMahon, K. and Barrett, J. E. (2003) *Getting Dressed,* London: Random House Children's Books. (A board book in which Elmo, along with the babies and toddlers, gets a variety of clothes so everybody is dressed for all kinds of weather.)

Merritt, K. (2006) *Night, Night, Baby,* London: Ladybird books. (A rhyming flap book with the words in the title appearing on every page. Caution: the flaps are big but are too vulnerable for repeated use with very young babies. Board book.)

📖 Smee, N. (2005) *Sleepyhead,* London: Mantra Lingua. (Gentle story of a sleepy baby: ten tired fingers, ten tired toes, two tired eyelids, one tired nose. Dual-language texts available.)

📖 Stockham, J. (2006) *Tucking In! Just Like Me!* Swindon: Child's Play. (The children find out that they eat just like baby animals. The mouse eats oats, the baby eats porridge; the lamb drinks milk from its mother and so does the baby. Breastfeeding shown in a natural way. Board book with fold-out-flaps.)

📖 Tofts, H. (2001) *I Eat Vegetables!* Slough: Zero to Ten. (A colourful photograph of a vegetable with its name on the opposite page; it is made clear which vegetables need peeling before eating.)

📖 —— (2001) *I Eat Fruit!* Slough: Zero to Ten. (A colourful photograph of a piece of fruit with its name on the opposite page; it is made clear which fruit needs peeling before eating.)

From 16–36 months

Development matters

- Show a desire to help with dress and hygiene routines.

- Communicate preferences.

- Seek to do things for themselves, knowing that an adult is close by, ready to support and help if needed.

- Become more aware that choices have consequences.

- Take pleasure in personal hygiene including toileting.

Key words

communicate preferences, engagement in hygiene and dressing routines

Main story: *The Best Blanket*
(S. Nash (2005), Tamarind, Northwood)

Most children have a special comforter, and Donna's was her old woollen blanket made up of knitted multicoloured squares. One day, Mum picked it up and suggested they wash it because it was so smelly, but Donna responded swiftly and, one sensed, with not a little panic. She said, 'No', very firmly, quickly establishing her rights over her own possessions. Then her dad said it was worn out. He wanted to throw it away and buy a new one, but Donna wouldn't hear of it. She said she would keep her blanket for ever. It was indeed very useful. When it was cold, she used it for a scarf. When it was windy, she held it above her head like a sail. When necessary, she used it as a bag to carry things and spread it out on the ground to lie on and pretend it was an island when she was feeling lonely. On camping trips, it became the roof of her tent, and she always cuddled up with it when she went to sleep; it even looked after her when she was scared. To Donna, it was the best blanket in the whole world, and she was not about to relinquish it.

This story could help to open up discussion about the comforters the children have and why they are so special to them but could also give the children ideas for role play and provide opportunities to talk about hygiene.

Activities

As young children develop, they will be increasingly eager to become independent and to take control of their own self-care.

- Children should be encouraged to fetch their own shoes and put on their coats. Support may be needed with getting arms into coat sleeves and doing up buttons, zips and shoelaces, but all of these skills can be practised in the setting. Produce a colourful cloth bag that has a number of pockets with different fastenings. You can hide various treasures in the pockets, so children are rewarded for managing to undo the fastener. A shoe can be nailed to a piece of wood, so that the children can practise tying laces or doing up buckles, although most shoes now for very young children are fastened with Velcro, which is more straightforward but needs a fair amount of strength to operate.

- As children become more aware of the choices available to them, they will want to be involved in the decisions concerning the food they are being offered and what they are to wear.

- Try and avoid mealtimes becoming a battleground. This is often easier said than done, even for an experienced practitioner. Some choice of the staple foods with which the children are familiar is a positive beginning. Religious and cultural regulations must be adhered to, and it is not good enough to provide solely vegetarian food, for example, for Muslim children, just because it is too much bother to get hold of halal meat. Children need to be provided with a healthy balanced diet, but there must be an element of choice within the different food types. Remember that toddlers often eat less than when they were babies. A six-month-old baby may gain two pounds (one kilogram) every eight weeks, but a toddler will not grow nearly as fast and may take six months to gain the same amount. Bear in mind that healthy children will eat when they are hungry and will not starve through refusing to eat. Toddlers often have times when they will only eat certain foods, but their favourites of the moment will quickly be exchanged for something else. These fads are not likely to threaten children's health and do not mean that they will not eventually eat a balanced diet.

- Some children will be dressed in a more formal way than others, and there will need to be a discussion with parents and carers concerning the implications of the type of clothing appropriate for messy activities and safe for playing in.

- Two-year-olds can become very fussy about what they want to put on, and by three are able to make a very good attempt at dressing themselves, although on occasions they might forget an item and arrive at the setting without their underpants. All such efforts should be praised.

- Toilet-training is an area in which close communication with parents and carers is vital, as there are cultural differences in the way this is tackled. In some countries, nappies would not traditionally be used at all. Toddlers would have open garments that they pull aside to urinate or defecate. This appears to be a highly efficient method. Something of a difficulty is developing in this country in that disposable nappies (for environmental reasons recyclable versions should be used, or reusable towelling versions) have now been designed in such a way that the baby does not feel as wet and uncomfortable as they once did. They do not, therefore, feel the same urgent need to be rid of their nappies as they did in the past. Some children will have been taught to stand or squat on a toilet seat. In some cultures, men as well as women sit on the toilet, so urinals will be particularly strange to some little boys. Boys are more likely to encounter urinals in school than in the nursery, and this will be different from home for all boys. Be aware that communal toileting areas for boys and girls may be unacceptable to some parents and carers.

Look, listen and note

- Keep records of children's achievements in all aspects of feeding or dressing themselves, and in toilet training. Choices of what to wear in the morning will be made at home, but these can be noted and discussed in the setting. 'Oh, you've decided to wear your blue trainers today. They look very smart. Why did you choose them today? Can you put them on yourself now? Oh, well done!'

- Note other examples of children's growing independence. They might fetch their coat from the peg, play happily on their own, or help clear up after snack time.

- Watch when choices are presented to children. This might be when activities are being discussed at the beginning of the day. Are the children able to make a decision about what to do first? If they are unable to communicate this verbally, are they able to point to a picture of the activity or in some other way indicate their preference?

Effective practice

Encourage and praise all efforts of the children to participate in their own self-care whether it be to feed themselves, fetch their own shoes, or pull up their pants after using the toilet. This is usually not difficult as children of this age are interested in, and keen to explore, everything. If their achievements are celebrated by supportive adults, this provides them with an even greater incentive to develop their skills.

Planning and resourcing

Make sure that children have:

- time to complete a task, so that they do not get unnecessarily frustrated or anxious.

- the appropriate utensils to enable them to feed themselves and to drink independently, while being aware that in some cultures, fingers are used for all meals by adults and children alike.

- the opportunity to plant a bulb, build a den, feed the hamster, choose a story or select a toy from the catalogue for the setting to buy.

- protective clothing for all weathers, so that outdoor activities can be accessed as often as indoor ones. To deny toddlers the joy of splashing in puddles would indeed be unforgivable!

- the chance to indicate a preference in their first language or non-verbally, if necessary, by providing an object or a picture to which they can point.

- access to stories that talk about the consequences that result from actions (see below *Wash Your Hands,* or *Big Smelly Bear*), and how the choice in one area may exclude participation in another.

Home links

Eating, toileting and dressing routines and the use of comforters are very personal, but also there may be wider implications that need to be taken into account. For example, religious and cultural restrictions must be respected by practitioners:

- Children may have clothing that covers certain parts of their bodies, and there may be issues around their being undressed in a public place. Discussions will have to take place concerning the implications of the type of clothing that is appropriate for the activities in the setting. Reasons for parents and carers not wanting their children to participate in particular activities should not be assumed by practitioners. It may be that the need for sand play has been appreciated by the parents and carers but that sand in the hair of African or African-Caribbean heritage children is irritating for them and very difficult to remove. In such a case, the wearing of their protective sun caps while playing in the sand may well provide a simple solution. Parents and carers should be asked to provide clothing suitable for cold, wet and sunny weather so their children can fully participate in all the activities provided by the setting.

- There may be cultural differences in the parents' and carers' attitude to their children's growth towards independence. In some countries, three- and four-year-olds look after the family livestock and by six or seven can strip a tractor and put it back together again! In others, the children are pampered in the early years and then on their sixth or seventh birthday are considered to be 'grown up' and able to take care of themselves. A friendly conversation is often the best way to get to the bottom of any concerns. When a climate of trust has been built up, all those involved, at home and in the setting, are more likely to be able to accommodate each other's preferences while maintaining respect for each other's beliefs and opinions.

Additional stories

Alborough, J. (1999) *Whose Socks Are Those?* Cambridge Mass.: Candlewick Press. (A group of curious animals investigate various items hanging on a clothesline and try to decide to whom each item belongs.)

Andreae, G. (2005) *Pants,* Oxford: David Fickling. (All sorts of sizes and shapes of brightly coloured pants worn on various parts of the body by all kinds of different animals.)

Cabrera, J. (2007) *Mummy, Carry Me Please,* London: Pinwheel. (All kinds of different creatures from crocodiles to spiders are carried in a variety of ways by their mothers.)

Clark, E. C. (2006) *I Love You, Blue Kangaroo,* London: Andersen Press. (Blue Kangaroo is a little girl's first comforter, but he is gradually sidelined as other soft toys arrive. In the end, he finds solace with the new baby. However, when the little girl discovers what's happened, she retrieves Blue Kangaroo because he is still very special.)

Cook, T. (2004) *Catch,* London: Scholastic Hippo. (Playing catch with Mum, Kiona gets disheartened because a ball is too big for her to catch and a berry is too small. Then her mum finds something she can catch – a kiss!)

Miller, V. (1991) *On Your Potty,* London: Walker Books. (Bartholomew bear insists he does not need his potty, 'Nah', but knows when the time is right and just makes it!)

Murphy, J. (2002) *A Piece of Cake,* London: Walker Books. (Mrs Large decides that she is too fat, so she puts the whole family on a diet, but when a large cake arrives for them one morning, the temptation is unbearable.)

Roddie, S. (1997) *Toes Are to Tickle,* London: Frances Lincoln. (This story follows a toddler and his little sister through the routines of their day, bringing in meal times, dressing, bathing and sleeping, as well as lots of fun times in between, both out of doors and inside, on their own and with their mum and dad.)

Ross, T. (2000) *Wash Your Hands,* London: Andersen Press. (The Little Princess is constantly reminded to wash her hands after playing outside, after touching the dog, using the potty, sneezing or else germs will get into her food and make her sick.)

—— (2008) *I Want My Potty,* London: Andersen Press. (Potty training the Little Princess proves to be an amusing business.)

—— (2008) *I Want to Be Tall!* London: Andersen Press. (The Little Princess needs to get her space hopper down from the apple tree, but she's too small, so she sets about doing all the things that are supposed to make her grow, but nothing seems to work. However, when her baby cousin arrives, she realise that she is not that small after all.)

Segal, J. (2006) *Carrot Soup,* London: Simon & Schuster Children's Books. (Rabbit has carefully prepared his carrot crop but is dismayed when he goes to harvest them to find someone has been there before him and has taken them all. No one can help, and he returns home sad and hungry, only to find that his friends have secretly prepared his favourite dish – carrot soup.)

Smee, N. (2007) *No Bed Without Ted,* London: Bloomsbury. (A little girl won't go to bed without her teddy bear. Children will enjoy searching with her by looking under all the flaps. Board book.)

Teckentrup, B. (2007) *Big Smelly Bear,* London: Frances Lincoln. (Big Smelly Bear is determined not to wash until he gets an itch he cannot reach. A big fluffy bear offers to help, but only on the condition that he has a bath first.)

Yasuo, O. and Watanabe, S. (1991) *How Do I Put It On?* London: Putnam Publishing Group. (A little boy tries to dress himself, but at first puts his clothes on the wrong parts of his body, for example, his pants on his head.)

From 30–60+ months

Development matters

- Show willingness to tackle problems and enjoy self-chosen challenges.

- Demonstrate a sense of pride in own achievement.

- Take initiatives and manage developmentally appropriate tasks.

- Operate independently within the environment and show confidence in linking up with others for support and guidance.

- Appreciate the need for hygiene.

Early learning goals

- Dress and undress independently and manage their own personal hygiene.

- Select and use activities and resources independently.

Key words

personal hygiene, choice of activities, pride in achievements

Main story: *My Wobbly Tooth Must Not Ever Fall Out*
(L. Child (2007), Puffin Books, London)

Lola is adamant that she wants to keep all her teeth and is most anxious that her wobbly one stays put. Her brother and sister try to explain that everyone loses their first teeth so that they can grow stronger ones. One day, her friend Lotta comes to play and tells Lola that her tooth has come out. Lola is then enlightened about the tooth fairy. Lotta had bought a chicken for their farm with the coin that was left under her pillow. Lola now can't wait for her tooth to come out, so she can buy a giraffe for their farm. She puts the tooth under her pillow, but then disaster strikes. She loses her tooth just before bedtime. She hunts high and low but to no avail. Lola thinks all is lost until her mum suggests that she goes to bed and dreams happy dreams so that she will smile and the tooth fairy will see the gap in her teeth. All goes to plan, and she buys her giraffe. Now she and Lotta can't wait to get some more wobbly teeth, so they can buy other animals for their farm.

This story should be comforting for children coming up to the stage when they will begin to lose their milk teeth. This can be a traumatic concept for some children, and it will help to be able to talk about it together. Conversations can be linked to the need for dental health in the form of eating less sugary foods, cleaning their teeth and visiting the dentist regularly (see *Sahir Goes to the Dentist* and *Molly at the Dentist,* details below).

Activities

- A number of stories deal with health issues and the need for taking care of ourselves. The children's interest in their own bodies and their growing sense of independence can be harnessed to help them establish such important practices as cleaning their teeth and washing their hands after certain activities, such as after going to the toilet, before eating, after coughing and sneezing, or after playing with their pets.

- Stories about routine visits to the dentist can be useful, and those dealing with a child seeing the doctor or going into hospital can be reassuring. A doctor's visit is likely to be made when children are not feeling well, or when they have to have an injection, so some understanding and discussion of how the doctor helps us is necessary. To see another child surviving the experience of going into hospital and being made better can encourage them. Some of these stories go into a lot of detail and should be helpful in explaining to children exactly what will happen. (See *Say Aah! My First Visit to the Doctor, Nita Goes to Hospital* and *Going to Hospital,* details below.)

- Dressing up in all its various forms is particularly interesting for children of this age. They are becoming increasingly independent in terms of dressing and undressing themselves, and one of the most stimulating provisions for the setting is one of the simplest to provide, namely the dressing-up box. This need not be packed full of tailor-made costumes in which the child can only be a nurse, a police officer or Spiderman. Such costumes may have a place in helping a child to play initially by providing an instant storyline, but if they stay with such a garment, their imagination can be stifled, and they may never progress. Far more inspiring is a mass of material of all shapes, sizes, colours, patterns and textures. Think of Donna's blanket (*The Best Blanket*) and all the variety of things it became. Think too of African women's traditional garment with the outer length of cloth wrapped round their middle. Twenty or more different uses have been identified for this one piece of material from strapping a baby to their back to carrying their lunch and drying up the dishes. Of course, shoes must not be forgotten as they provide a particular fascination for children, and 'shoes' is often one of the first words they say. They like their own shoes, and shoes in the dressing-up box can be the cause of a certain amount of friction, although children who have been given the skills to sort out their own conflicts can sometimes reach some surprising resolutions, like the story of the two little girls who both wanted to wear a pair of glittery shoes but who decided to wear one each. Not a solution an interfering adult would have come up with, but one with which they were both entirely happy.

- In terms of their everyday clothes, there will be a lot of interest in looking at each other's clothes, and, in a small group, children can identify the items of clothing they are wearing, both for inside and for outside use, and a number of activities can be organised around this:

    - Any number of action rhymes can focus on articles of clothing. For example, 'If you're wearing trousers, pat your knees.' 'If your shoes have Velcro, stamp your feet'. Then the colour of a jumper, for example, can become a verse of a song to the tune of 'Peter Hammers with Two Hammers'. For example, 'Charlotte's wearing green socks, green socks, green socks, Charlotte's wearing green socks, all day long.'

    - Sitting in a circle, the children take off one shoe and place it in a pile in the centre. Look together at the one shoe the children still have on. Study each one in turn and talk about anything different or special about it. (If you have children with particularly shabby footwear, which might embarrass them, then an alternative would be to get the children to choose a pair of shoes each from the dressing-up box to use for the game.) The children then in turn find another child's missing shoe from the centre while the others sing a rhyme similar to 'Little Betty Blue Has Lost Her Shoe'. For example, 'Eunjoo Choi has lost her shoe. Can William Murray find it?'

- It provides an opportunity to talk about why we need to wear clothes, while animals and birds do not, and what types of clothes are suitable for different kinds of weather. You can make up a story about a boy and girl and what clothes they needed when they walked to nursery in the rain, went swimming, went to dancing classes, played in their den, played in a sunny garden, or built snowchildren.

Look, listen and note

- Observe the children's developing ability to follow up ideas they have for their own play and how they put these ideas into practice. Note how successful they are, and the ways in which they celebrate their achievements.

- Note the children's choices in terms of their selection of appropriate clothing for different activities. Do they get an apron before painting or going to the water tray and return it when they have finished? Do they dress appropriately for the weather conditions if they are going outside?

Effective practice

Having talked about problem-solving with the children, give them the time and opportunity to sort out their own dilemmas, whether it be in terms of equipment needed for a particular game or an argument with a friend. Create an ethos of care but not a care that smothers, rather one that

143

frees the children to grow, to make their own mistakes and to celebrate their own achievements. Let them know that you value their efforts and are there to support and encourage them, when necessary, but are also ready to step back and allow them to continue independently, when they are ready.

Planning and resourcing

Allow the children to participate as much as possible in the choice of activities and equipment that are made available in the setting. Sometimes, for example, the organisation of the room(s) will be solely adult-initiated, but at other times it is important to build on the children's ideas. Always strive for a balance between familiar activities that the children can return to again and again to practise their skills and new ideas to challenge and stimulate their imagination. The adult presence is still vital to make sure that there are opportunities for them to remember and celebrate their achievements and to provide support for the action that is just outside their grasp, but which tomorrow they will be able to tackle alone.

Home links

- Parents and carers and practitioners should always keep each other up to date with matters relating to health and safety generally and in particular with any health concerns or medical conditions that require treatment or special observation. Allergies of all kinds need to be catered for and concerns shared about suspected hearing or visual impairment, speech and language difficulties, or any special educational need. Learning English as an additional language does not in itself constitute a learning difficulty as defined by the Code of Practice for Special Educational Needs (2001). The ability to speak another language should be viewed as an asset, not as a problem.

- Parents and carers are a great resource for providing materials for the dressing-up box. Materials from all round the world will make a marvellous array of colour and excitement and will stimulate all sorts of play and, as off cuts from clothes-making or old scarves and petticoats are particularly welcome, no one need feel that what they have to contribute is not acceptable.

Additional stories

Barkow, H. (2005) *Nita Goes to Hospital,* London: Mantra Lingua. (Nita breaks her leg and has to be taken to hospital, so she has to be brave. This story is gently reassuring and should allay the fears of a child who has to go into hospital. Available in English and more than twenty-five bilingual editions.)

Civardi, A. (2005) *Going to Hospital,* London: Usborne Publishing. (Ben has to go into hospital for an ear operation. His family support him, and the whole process is followed through in the story, beginning with the initial visit to see the doctor. This would be very helpful for any child having to go in to hospital.)

Child, L. (2007) *I Will Never Eat a Tomato,* London: Orchard Books. (Lola will not eat a whole variety of foods until her brother finds a way to change their status. When peas become green drops from Greenland and carrots orange twiglets from Jupiter, they are quite acceptable. Pop-up.)

Coplans, P. (2003) *Spaghetti for Suzy,* London: Andersen Press. (Suzy would only eat spaghetti until she met a cat who used a strand to make a fishing line, a pig who used it for shoe laces and a dog who knitted with it. To say thank you, they each gave her some fruit, which she felt obliged to eat but then decided that it was almost as good as spaghetti.)

French, V. (1995) *Oliver's Vegetables,* London: Hodder Children's Books. (Oliver will only eat chips until he plays a game with his grandpa. Whatever vegetable he finds, he eats that night. By the end of the week, his diet is far more extensive.)

145

—— (1998) *Oliver's Fruit Salad,* London: Hodder Children's Books. (Oliver remembers the fresh fruit that he picked with his grandpa and will not eat the canned and packaged fruit his mother provides.)

Gardiner, L. (2006) *You Can Do It, Lola!* Oxford: Oxford University Press. (Marcie's dog, Lola, is eating too much of the wrong sort of food and, as a consequence, is putting on so much weight that she can hardly squeeze into her kennel. So a regime of healthy eating and exercise is introduced, and Lola succeeds with a little help from her friends.)

Green, J. (1999) *I'm Special,* London: Hodder Wayland. (A focus on three different disabilities through the day-to-day experiences of disabled children.)

—— (2001) *Say Aah! My First Visit to the Doctor,* London: Hodder Wayland. (Told by a little boy in the first person with lively illustrations. The whole process is covered: feeling ill, going to the doctor, going to the chemist and then bouncing back to health, literally.)

Gretz, S. (1999) *Rabbit Food,* London: Walker Books. (Grandpa Rabbit comes to stay and gets his young grandson to eat up his vegetables, but the little rabbits soon discover that their grandpa doesn't eat his carrots.)

Hest, A. (2002) *Don't You Feel Well, Sam?* London: Walker Books. (Sam is a little bear with a bad cough, but Mrs Bear can't get him to take his medicine until she mentions the fact that there is snow on the way.)

Hutchings, P. (1999) *You'll Soon Grow into Them, Titch,* London: Tandem Library. (Titch always has hand-me-downs from his older brother and sister, but one day his mother decides that he needs some brand-new clothes and, for once, he gets to pass his clothes on and to assure someone else that they will grow into them.)

Moses, B. (1997) *'I'll Do It!' Taking Responsibility,* Hove: Wayland Publishers. (The children are asked questions all the way through about whether they take responsibility for their self-care and whether they can be trusted to look after a baby sister, a pet, run errands, help after an accident, take care of their own and other people's possessions and take on important jobs at school. The focus is a little boy who sometimes gets it right!)

Petty, C. (2005) *Sahir Goes to the Dentist,* London: Mantra Lingua. (Sahir loses a tooth, and his dad takes him to the dentist with his sister, Yasmin, who it transpires has a small hole in one of her teeth. Both children are shown how to care for their teeth. Available in English and more than twenty bilingual editions.)

Petty, K. (2007) *Hair,* London: Frances Lincoln. (Wearing different hairstyles for a variety of occasions, around the world.)

Quarmby, K. (2008) *Fussy Freya,* London: Frances Lincoln. (Freya decides she doesn't like the food her mother is providing and becomes very thin indeed until Grandma Clare takes her in hand and Freya learns a lesson she will never forget!)

Robertson, M. P. (2001) *The Egg,* London: Frances Lincoln. (George finds himself rearing a baby dragon and making a very good job of it too, but after a while the dragon begins to pine for its own kind and then disappears.)

Sage, A. (2007) *Molly at the Dentist,* London: Gullane Children's Books. (Molly is a little green dinosaur, and when she finally has two teeth, she makes her first visit to the dentist, but she won't open her mouth for Dr Brushwell at first. However, when he gives her a little mirror so she can see into her mouth as well, she is won round and is soon enjoying brushing her teeth with her new toothbrush.)

Tarpley, N. A. (2004) *I Love My Hair,* London: Little, Brown & Company. (A little girl of African-Caribbean heritage talks about her hair, including a description of how it is washed, oiled, combed and styled.)

Teague, K. (1991) *Imran's Clinic,* Hayes: Magi Publications. (Imran visits the clinic when his baby brother has an injection. He meets his culturally diverse friends there and afterwards they make a clinic at Anna's house.)

Persona Doll story

Introduce the Persona Doll over a number of sessions before talking about an issue.

Meet Tomasz

Tomasz lives with his mum, who is English, and his dad, who is Polish. His mum met his dad when she went to a country called Poland to teach English. Tomasz is five years old, and he has an older sister called Juliana, who is seven years old and a baby sister, Anna, who is one month old. They live in a semi-detached house, which is where two houses are joined together. (*Does anyone here live in a semi-detached house?*)

Mum is a schoolteacher now, and, before Anna was born, she taught in the primary school that Tomasz and Juliana go to. Juliana was in her class last year, and Tomasz might be next year, or he might go into Mrs Robinson's class instead. Mum says Mrs Robinson is a very good teacher. Tomasz's dad is an electrician, and he mends cookers and heaters and puts new wires into people's houses so that everything is kept safe. (*Can you think of all the things in your house that need electricity, all the things that have a plug and have to be switched on before they can work?*)

Mum and Dad try to speak Polish at home, so that Juliana and Tomasz and Anna will grow up speaking two languages. It is quite hard because everything else is in English, at school and on the television, and Juliana and Tomasz are better at speaking that language, but in the summer they are going to Poland for the first time to meet Dad's family. They are really excited and are practising their Polish so they can speak to their grandparents and to all their cousins, because Dad has two brothers and two sisters, and they all have children. (*How many people have you got in your family?*) Mum said their school is going to get some stories written in other languages with English, so they will be able to borrow the Polish–English ones to take home and read together, then Dad can help them. He went to school in Poland and when he was sixteen he went to a technical college where he learnt to be an electrician. When Tomasz's dad lived in Poland, he went to the Catholic Church every Sunday with all the family, but Dad doesn't go much now, only at Christmas and Easter time. Then they all go together; Tomasz likes it. The church is very beautiful with lots of coloured

Tomasz

glass pictures in the windows and candles and smelly smoke, although that sometimes makes him cough. Tomasz finds it hard to understand his dad sometimes. One day, Tomasz was excited because another boy from Poland had came into his class, and he had made friends with Pawel, although he could not speak Polish very well because he spoke Romani at home. When Dad found out he was a Roma, he said that Tomasz was not to play with him anymore because Pawel would not work hard and would get him into trouble. Tomasz was sad about this, and he knew that Mum and Dad had quarrelled about it, because he heard them shouting at night when he went to bed.

Tomasz likes to watch football with his dad, and sometimes they go to watch Manchester United because they live in Trafford. It costs a lot of money to buy a season ticket, so they can only go now and again, but they watch the matches on television. (*Do you watch football at home? What do you like to watch on the television?*) Tomasz also goes to ballet with his sister; there are a few boys in the class, but mostly they are girls. Tomasz used to go with his mum when she took Juliana, and he would sit and watch. One day the teacher asked him if he would like to join in. He felt a bit silly at first, but soon he was enjoying it. He liked the music, and he found he was very good at dancing. Everyone who does ballet has to be very fit, and the boys especially need to be very strong so they can lift the girls in the air. When he's older, Tomasz wants to go to the gym with his mum. At the moment, he just goes to the school gym club and football practice, so that keeps him fit.

Mum tries to give them healthy food to eat at home. Tomasz's dad likes Polish food, and so does his mum. Dad makes their tea a lot at the moment to help Mum because baby Anna is still very new. Tomasz loves it when they have smoked sausage and pickled cucumbers, and his favourite pudding is *sernik,* which is Polish cheesecake. He likes pasta, too, and bananas. (*What are your favourite foods?*) Juliana and Tomasz try to help Mum, too. They can both wash themselves now and clean their teeth and get dressed, although Tomasz still finds it hard to do up the zip on his anorak. (*What do you find difficult? Can you get dressed and undressed yourself? Can you show me how you clean your teeth? And brush your hair?*) Everyone is rather tired at the moment because baby Anna still wakes up in the night and cries a lot. Tomasz is disappointed because he thought he would be able to play with her, but she is so small and noisy, and she can't even talk yet. Mum is very busy with the baby, too, and sometimes he feels that she loves the new baby more than him. (*Have any of you got a baby at home? Do you know what Tomasz feels like? Could you help him? What should he do?*)

In school, Tomasz's friends call him Tom for short, and he is happy with that. He likes to read stories and to play in the tree house. (*What do you like to do the most?*) He has a best friend called Sarah who goes to his ballet class. Sarah likes to climb too, and they go to gym club together. She wears glasses, which is difficult sometimes, especially at gym club and when she's dancing because she has to take them off, and then she can't see so well. Tomasz told her that she'll be able to have contact lenses like his mum when she's bigger.

Sometimes Tomasz gets teased at school because one of the boys saw him at the ballet class and told the others. Some of the boys called him a sissy and say he is like a girl. They don't know how strong Tomasz has to be to do dancing. (*How do you think Tomasz feels when they call him a sissy? What should he do about it?*) They tease Sarah, too, because she wears glasses. (*How do you think Sarah feels when they say her glasses look funny? What can she do about it?*)

Tomasz is very glad that he came to see you today; you've been very helpful. Could he come and see you another day and tell you about his trip to Poland, and hear about your holidays?

The EYFS principles

The EYFS principles are grouped into four themes that are concerned with the individual needs of the child, the importance of building positive relationships and the need for the adults in the setting to create an environment that enables the child to learn and to develop to the best of their ability. As these themes relate to this section on self-care, they are specifically about helping children to gain a sense of self-respect and concern for their own personal hygiene and care and how they can develop independence. As babies move into early childhood, those aspects of their care that have been performed entirely by the caring adults around them are gradually taken over by the young children. With praise and encouragement, they will thrive on the challenges of being able to care for themselves. They will develop the skills necessary to nourish and clothe themselves and to keep themselves clean. As they learn to make decisions, they will begin to recognise that these have consequences.

The way these caring routines were introduced in the past was heavily influenced by family, cultural and religious traditions, and in close-knit communities this is still the case. However, in environments where the nuclear family is more isolated, and parents and carers rely more on professional help, there has been a greater reliance on books on child care, and each different generation has followed its own guru. Either way, there are strong opinions voiced on what is the right and wrong way to nurture a young child. If the adults in the setting and those in the home are to teach children self-respect, then they must have respect for each other's views and seek to work together for the good of the children. Matters of health and cleanliness are of paramount concern for all those who care for the children. If there are worries about the way the children are helped to become knowledgeable and independent in such matters, then these must be taken seriously by everyone, and each must be prepared to humbly accept that they might have something to learn from the other. The children need to build positive relationships with adults at home and in the setting who together can create an environment where they receive trustworthy models, steady support for their own attempts to care for their personal needs and where their achievements are valued and celebrated. Only then can they truly thrive.

6 Sense of community

From birth–20 months

> ### *Development matters*
>
> - Respond to differences in their environment, for example, showing excitement or interest.
>
> - Learn that special people are a source of sustenance, comfort and support.
>
> - Learn that their voice and actions have effects on others.
>
> ### *Key words*
>
> special people, effect on others

Main story: *My Body – A First Board Book*
(D. Murrell (ed.) (2003), Picthall and Gunzi, Bromley)

This little book features photographs of a group of toddlers and very young children from a variety of ethnic backgrounds. Each two-page spread has an overall title, and labels are attached as appropriate. The themes include body parts (in detail over six pages), the senses, different hair (although the red hair is only faintly so), eight facial expressions, ways to make a noise, a daily routine, getting dressed, modelling home play and physical actions

153

with an interactive part that asks the reader, 'Can you ...?' I particularly like the last two-page spread that is entitled, 'Let's match!' There are different body parts to match up: two pictures of a foot, a mouth, an eye, a nose, fingers, eyelashes, an eyebrow, a fingernail and a hand. There are different skin tones used throughout, and the reader is asked to 'Point to the two hands!' 'Find the two eyebrows! 'Match the two feet!' Sections of this book would also be useful for other areas of personal, social and emotional development.

Activities

- Provide babies with plenty of opportunities to experience different environments: outside play on the grass and in the sandpit, as well as inside on the carpet. They need to encounter quiet spaces as well as stimulating noisier environments.

- Provide different types of items to interest babies and encourage them to explore: things that roll, spin, rock, float; things that are hard and can be struck with an implement; things that are soft that they can snuggle into; things that are shiny, dull or brightly coloured; things that are tough, such as stainless-steel bowls, or vulnerable such as bubbles.

- As a key person for the children, give them your full attention during the daily routines of feeding, nappy changing and sleeping, and be aware of times when they need support to learn a new skill. Let them know that they are valued and that they belong to the community of the setting as well as to their home.

- Play 'Peep-Boo'-type games but with puppets, dolls or soft toys of different colours and shapes. Some might be wearing glasses (use frames with no lenses, or unbreakable plastic lenses). Your presence will provide the security and comfort to the young children and give them the confidence to face anything that looks different.

Look, listen and note

- Note the babies' responses to difference in their immediate sur-roundings. Are they anxious about something different, or excited and interested and keen to explore?

- As they become aware of the different children and adults around them, observe their responses to those with whom they come into contact. Do they experiment with using their voice and seeing what effect they have on others? Do they test their actions by looking to you for your reactions? How do they respond if you are encouraging, or discouraging of the action?

Effective practice

- If brothers and sisters are in the same setting, they can come and spend some time with the baby and you can talk to the baby afterwards about the games they played together. 'Oh, you like your sister, Matt; she reads you lots of your favourite stories.'

- Towards the end of this stage, toddlers will recognise people they know very well from a photograph, and you can talk to them about parents and carers and older brothers and sisters.

  - Where's Daddy? Can you see him? Yes, that's right, Daddy gives you a ride on his shoulders.

  - Oh, there's your friend, Oliver, what is he doing? Shall we go and see?

  - Here's a big ball. I'll kick it to you. Can you kick it back? Well done!

- Significant places are useful for conversation too.

  - I know you like to sit under the tree, the leaves are so pretty aren't they? Can you see the sunshine coming through? Put your hands here and catch the light.

- Your room at home looks very exciting. Mummy says you have pictures of teddy bears on your wall; some are blue and some are pink and some are green. I know you like to take monkey with you when you go to bed. He's very special isn't he?

Planning and resourcing

- Make sure that babies have a good view of life all around. There is so much going on in the setting, and the great variety of activities will intrigue and stimulate them, even though they are not old enough to participate in many of them. They will be watching how to open a door, how to ride a bike, what fun it is to paint a picture. They will witness laughter and tears, shrieks of joy and of pain and will be trying to make sense of it all. They will see people of all different shapes and sizes in a vast variety of clothing with loud and soft voices, with dark brown skin and light pink skin, with long and short straight hair, long and short curly hair, and every length in between. Some will come close to them and talk to them and care for them and smile at them; some will watch them from a distance.

- Provide all different kinds of food, but make sure that most will be familiar to them according to their cultural background. Encourage them to experience new tastes, as long as these are acceptable to their family, and to express their likes and dislikes.

- Make sure that you enable the children to follow the cultural and religious observances of their family and help them to learn to respect these.

Home links

- Be careful to observe family views and opinions on physical contact and to find out the different meaning of particular gestures, particularly ones that are offensive.

- Find out the parents' and carers' views on leaving a baby to cry. Some will never do this and may feel distressed if they think that their child is left to cry for a long time in the setting.

- Encourage parents to teach their child's key person a few lullabies that they use at home. These may be in a language other than English but are likely to be simple. Tapes of some of these songs could be used alongside to support the practitioners in their learning of these soothing sounds.

- Encourage parents and carers to share aspects of their clothing or food with the other children in the setting so they can begin to celebrate difference and not to fear it.

- Find out the key festivals celebrated by the families and incorporate these into the activities in the setting. Zucker has written many books for young children about all the major festivals. A selection is below, but there are many more that you can share with the children.

Additional stories

Anholt, C. and Anholt, L. (2006) *Big Book of Little Children,* London: Walker Books. (A focus on little children from around the world exploring the things they like and dislike, their feelings, their favourite activities and their families.)

Brooks, J. (2008) *My First Prayers,* London: Frances Lincoln. (Fifteen prayers for various times of the day from around the world for very young children.)

McKee, D. (1998) *Elmer's Friends,* London: Milet Publishers. (Elmer's friends are all different, but in one respect they are the same! Available in English and more than twenty bilingual editions.)

Oxenbury, H. (1998) *Say Goodnight,* London: Walker Books. (A group of babies of various ethnic origins play together and say goodnight.)

Tadjo, V. (2000) *Grandma Nana,* London: Milet Publishing. (An African grandmother tells stories of wisdom and laughter to her grandchildren. A picture storybook with simple rhyming text.)

Zucker, J. (2003) *Apples and Honey: A Rosh Hashanah Story,* London: Frances Lincoln. (A simple introduction to the Jewish festival of Rosh Hashanah for pre-school children. It focuses on one family as they eat apples and honey, hear the *shofar* and plan for a sweet and joyful year ahead.)

—— (2005) *Lanterns and Firecrackers: A Chinese New Year Story,* London: Frances Lincoln. (A simple introduction to the New Year festivities for pre-school children. It focuses on one family as they let off firecrackers, light their lanterns and watch the amazing dragon dance.)

—— (2005) *Sweet Dates to Eat: A Ramadan and Eid Story,* London: Frances Lincoln. (A simple introduction to the Muslim season of Ramadan and Eid for pre-school children. It follows one family as they fast each day, go to the mosque on the Night of Power and then enjoy a delicious array of food at the beginning of Eid.)

—— (2008) *Lighting a Lamp: A Divali Story,* London: Frances Lincoln. (A simple introduction to the Hindu festival of Divali for pre-school children. It focuses on one family as they make *rangoli* patterns, light *divas* and watch a firework display.)

—— (2008) *Hope and New Life! An Easter Story,* London: Frances Lincoln. (A simple introduction to the Christian festival of Easter for pre-school children. It focuses on one family as they take Holy Communion, eat hot cross buns, go on an Easter-egg hunt and watch a big parade.)

From 16–36 months

Development matters

- Learn that they have similarities and differences that connect them to, and distinguish them from, others.

- Show a strong sense of self as a member of different communities, such as their family or setting.

- Show affection and concern for special people.

Key words

differences and similarities, sense of belonging

Main story: *My World, Your World*
(M. Walsh (2004), Picture Corgi of Random House Children's Books, London)

A vibrant book with colourful outlines and a simple accompanying text that describes the similarities and differences between children all around the world. It begins with a little girl against a green landscape with a blue sky and the text says, 'Kavita wears a colourful sari to school.' On the second page, against a snowy scene, we read, 'Jacob wears a warm jacket and snowboots. But …' Then on the third page, we see the legs of the two children wearing trainers, and the text says, 'they both wear trainers in gym club!' We then meet Georgie and Luc who greet others in a different language, but who both say, 'hee, hee, hee' when their feet are tickled. Prudence and Mai use different utensils to eat, but they both drink their juice through a straw. Muhib and Edie ride different animals, but they both ride skateboards in the park, and, finally, Max lives at the top of a block of flats and Ben lives in a farmhouse, but they both love looking at the stars! A delightful book to help the children to recognise and celebrate their similarities and their differences.

Activities

- Play games where the children have to name some one else. For example, you could turn 'Simon Says', into 'Melanie Says', and when it is time to change over, the child in the centre could name another child to go in the middle and perform an action for everyone to copy. Alternatively, in singing games such as, 'The Farmer's in His Den', you can introduce the idea of using someone's name instead of pointing to them when choosing the various characters (although this can still be used where a child is unable to communicate verbally).

- Use the children's interest in their clothes and their shoes to introduce descriptive terms, different shapes, colours and textures. They can then talk about things that are the same, 'My socks are the same colour as Tara's jumper', or different: 'My T-shirt has long sleeves, but Liam's has short sleeves.'

- Use the book, *All Kinds of People* (see below) to introduce a topic on ourselves. Look at similarities and differences in skin tone, hair colour, eye colour, height, weight, length of fingernails and size of feet and hands.

- Look at pictures of different kinds of houses, as well as looking at those in the neighbourhood. Talk about the similarities and differences between a bungalow and a flat, a terraced house and a trailer.

Look, listen and note

- Observe children's awareness of their individual features. Are they able to compare aspects of their physical appearance with those of their friends?

- Look out for children's identification of particular aspects of their dress. Do they tell you about their new shoes, point out a pattern on their shirt, or show you a motif on their jumper?

- Record whether children are able to ask about any differences they notice. Have you observed any learned behaviour of theirs that is discriminatory? Do they feel good about themselves? Do they consider themselves to be superior to any one else, or any group of people? If so, does that affect their behaviour towards those people? Do they feel inferior because of any aspect of their heritage or their family lifestyle?

Effective practice

- Always be ready to listen to the children and to let them know that it is all right to notice things that are different and it is fine to talk about them. The children need to share what is puzzling them; they need to make sense of a situation. Recently an eighteen-month-old, who had never seen a person with a darker skin tone, was observed playing with her dolls; she kept washing the black doll. All she knew was that when her hands were black, she was told they were dirty. An adult observing this behaviour was initially shocked thinking that the child had learned some racist behaviour, but we need to be careful in our reactions as these can sometimes result in conveying a message that this difference is something we do not talk about. As the child develops, she will need to be included in positive discussions about difference and helped to understand that we all have different skin tones, and that it is quite normal to have dark brown skin and it does not mean the person is dirty. If nothing is said, the child will continue to put her own construction on the situation.

- Talk to the children about their families, their friends and their local community. The children need to know that whatever their heritage, family structure, linguistic skills, abilities or disabilities, their family and their friends are welcomed by you and that their views and opinions are valued and respected. To be inattentive to the carers of the children, or to dismiss their languages, is to reject them.

- Help the child to form positive relationships with the community nurses, police officers, shopkeepers, doctors and health visitors by inviting them into the setting.

- Create your own Persona Doll stories based on the needs of the children in your setting and the community that you serve.

Planning and resourcing

Provide positive images of:

- the children, their families, their pets and the members of their community; use photographs to stimulate conversations about those represented, what they are doing, what they look like, what they enjoy;

- people from many different backgrounds in the storybooks and posters you buy for the setting, including those from different cultural backgrounds and religions, those who have particular physical disabilities or learning difficulties.

Examine all material for ethnic, social, gender and ability stereotyping and provide dual language books and story tapes, CDs and DVDs.

Home links

- Encourage the parents to be open with each other and to ask about things that puzzle them about each other's lifestyle. Those who feel embarrassed to ask about a particular aspect of another's life, or who are afraid of being misunderstood, might well ask the practitioner and expect them to be a go-between, but this can create more problems than it solves, although you may well want to facilitate the creation of a parents' and carers' group. If the adults are seen to be communicating freely and honestly, then the children will be more likely to follow their example.

- Encourage parents and carers to come into the setting more formally to share information about their special festivals, to bring in their celebratory food and decorations and to share their religious observances.

- Ask parents to record simple stories and songs in their first language to help their own child's first-language development and to share with the other children.

Additional stories

- Anholt, C. and Anholt, L. (2005) *Big Book of Families,* London: Walker Books. (A focus on different families from around the world.)

- Damon, E. (1995) *All Kinds of People,* London: Tango Books. (People come in all different shapes and sizes and have many different interests. A lift-the-flap book which is very useful for introducing a topic on ourselves.)

- Zucker, J. (2004) *It's Party Time! A Purim Story,* London: Frances Lincoln. (A simple introduction to the Jewish festival of Purim for pre-school children. It focuses on one family as they dress up, give presents and make lots of noise as they celebrate.)

From 30–60+ months

Development matters

- Make connections between different parts of their life experience.

- Have an awareness of, and an interest in, cultural and religious differences.

- Have a positive self-image and show that they are comfortable with themselves.

- Enjoy joining in with family customs and routines.

Early learning goals

- Understand that people have different needs, views, cultures and beliefs that need to be treated with respect.

- Understand that they can expect others to treat their needs, views, cultures and beliefs with respect.

Key words

cultural and religious differences, positive self-image

Main story: *Something Else*
(K. Cave (1995), Puffin Books, London)

Something Else lives all alone and has no friends. Wherever he goes, other groups of animals and birds say he doesn't belong with them, that he is 'Something Else'. He tries to do the things they do, but it doesn't work out. He looks different and cannot talk or play or even see things the way they do, so in the end he returns home on his own. Another creature knocks at his door and wants to stay, but Something Else says he was the wrong sort of Something Else and turns him away. Later he remembers how small and sad he had felt when the others had turned him away. He runs after the creature and asks him to stay. He says it doesn't matter that they are different. They become friends and do things together, and, later, when a boy knocks at the door, who is *really* different, they welcome him in without a word.

Ask the children questions such as:

- What did Someone Else feel like when the others said he didn't belong?
- What did he do about it?
- Did it work out?
- How do you feel if someone says you can't be their friend?
- How do you feel if someone says you can't play?
- What if someone says you don't talk like they do, or they can't understand what you say?
- Suppose someone says you look different and your food smells funny?
- What did Something Else do when the creature came into his house?
- Why did he send him away?
- How did the creature look? What did he do?
- Why did Something Else change his mind?
- Does it matter if we are different from someone else?
- What would it be like if we were all the same?
- What happens when the boy wants to be their friend?

Activities

All these activities should help children to celebrate their similarities and their differences.

- Involvement in cooking food from different traditions. Instead of having a project on bread, for example, why not expand it even more to include all the foods that are made from a basic cereal and water mix, and perhaps an egg? All kinds of crackers, chapattis, pancakes, crêpes, wafers and porridges from around the world can then be included. Eggs on their own form a part of many celebrations and can be coloured and their shells used to make mosaic patterns.

- Songs and rhymes from different cultures and in different languages are a fun way of helping children to appreciate someone else's language and culture, and they will enjoy learning to count in other languages.

- Walking for the first time into an environment where there are dual-language welcome posters and multilingual displays of the children's work sends out powerful messages to the children that we are all different and isn't it wonderful that we are. If we all looked exactly the same, did the same things, spoke in the same way, then we might as well be a lot of robots! Likewise, inclusion in the displays and reading materials of children who use wheelchairs or other aids will be affirming for children with those particular needs.

- Celebrate the festivals that are special to those in your setting. These might include birthday and New Year celebrations; the Jewish Passover, Hanukah, and Rosh Hashanah; the Sikh and Hindu festivals of Divali; the Muslim festival of Eid; the Christian festivals of Christmas and Easter. Find out, too, about other celebrations in order to give the children information about them. For example, if you wanted to introduce the children to some aspects of the 'Day of the Dolls' and you had no children from a Japanese background, you could use a Persona Doll to introduce the topic. If your Doll was from another culture, she could tell the children about her Japanese friend. The Doll could be wearing a kimono that her friend had lent her and could ask the children if they would like to try one on or make a paper one for their dolls. They could have tea together sitting on the floor, following the Japanese tradition. The serious aspects of remembering their ancestors could be shared too. Children may have grandparents who have died and can share some of their memories.

- A variety of instruments from different countries can be introduced to the children. Try to find out how and when these instruments are used. Some will be for general use, but others may be kept for very special occasions, and this should be respected. Maracas are very easy to make with rice or beans inside two glued-together yoghurt pots and decorated with coloured string wrapped tightly round the outside so the pots are no longer visible. It is easy then to make a loop at one end to carry the maracas or to hang them up when not in use.

- Patterns from around the world can be used for all kinds of art-work: Celtic tartans with coloured stripes crossing at right angles and African wood sculpture and bead patterns for necklaces and anklets which can be copied by the children. Colours have special significance in African art. For example, red can be used for sorrow, dissatisfaction or aggression; blue for tenderness; green for productiveness. Islamic art has some wonderful patterns; these have been developed to such a sophisticated level because images of living creatures are not to be represented. Some Muslim families may not have dolls in the house for this reason and may not encourage their children to draw pictures of themselves or their families, although photographs are commonly taken now, and such matters need to be discussed with individual families. In Indian art, the mango pattern has been popular for hundreds of years. Copied by Europeans, it is known here as Paisley after the Scottish town where it was imitated and printed on cloth. As with Aboriginal art, Native American art is believed to have power over its creators and is taken very seriously. Even very young children can create a simple pattern. It might be a starburst, a tessellation, or an irregular pattern but when their paper is placed alongside twenty others to make a wall display, the effect can be extraordinary.

- Instrumental music from around the world can also be used to create an atmosphere and may be used in conjunction with artwork from a particular country. Such music may be used to soothe or to stimulate; it may be familiar to children and make them feel at home, or it may be unfamiliar and stir their imagination.

- Fill the dressing-up box with as many pieces of materials as possible from different traditions so that a vast array of colours, patterns and textures can be experienced and used as the children wish for a myriad of purposes in their imaginative play.

Look, listen and note

- Note whether the children have a sense of belonging to their family, to their culture, to their religion. Record how this manifests itself. Do they enjoy hearing a story or know any songs in another language? Do they offer the name of a fruit or a food dish in their first language? Do the children copy the style of their relatives when they are dressing up? Are they happy to participate when their special festivals are being celebrated? How do they respond to those who are different from them? Can they understand such difference, and respect it? Observations of this kind will often pick up whether children are feeling isolated and want to fit in with the dominant culture, to be like everyone else. This could indicate a simple desire to belong to the new group, but it may be covering bullying, racist or otherwise, or discrimination by a staff member or the child's peers. Nothing may be said, but young children are particularly sensitive to atmosphere, and they will rely heavily on body language, especially if they are learning English as an additional language.

- Observe the children with particular disabilities. How far are they able to participate in the activities? Are they truly integrated into the community of the setting?

Effective practice

If a child is the only one from a particular cultural background, or with a particular disability, they may not want to be the centre of attention, but rather seek to blend in with the rest of the children. For this reason, I would not advocate using a Persona Doll that exactly mirrors those children's backgrounds or disabilities. Rather, their issues can be discussed by using a slightly different scenario about something that has happened elsewhere. The victim and the perpetrator of a particular action are then both freed up to talk about how the characters in the story are feeling and what can be done to help them. Hopefully, as a setting develops its ethos of acceptance and celebration of diversity, the children will begin to appreciate each other's abilities and talents and feel comfortable about sharing their own skills and anxieties.

Planning and resourcing

- Provide spaces and times for children to play alone, or to be quiet, as well as times for stimulating activity. The children need to make sense of the world around them and also to come to terms with who they are, as an individual, as part of a family, however that is structured, and as part of a community, both at home and in the setting.

- Each child is an individual and will need different support from the practitioner in order to fully participate in all the activities and to be able to communicate and make relationships with others. Some will be greatly assisted if they are provided with bilingual support to enable them to express their feelings and opinions and also for their first-language development. At best, this will be provided through a member of staff who shares their linguistic repertoire, but dual-language stories and songs on CD and on the computer will provide some support. All the children will appreciate resources that reflect their cultural background, while some will additionally need the provision of aids to enable them to lessen or overcome the effects of a physical disability or impairment. All the children will be helped by someone spending time with them and being prepared to listen and be patient with those who learn more slowly.

Home links

- Role-play areas need to include material from cultures around the world, and parents can be asked to donate various items. Lengths of material are often more flexible for the children to use than made-up costumes that suggest only one type of play. There may be particular patterns that are special to their community, and the parents can show the children examples of these.

- Parents and carers can be asked to tell stories and teach the children songs in their first language and to talk about their life in their country of origin, if they were not born in the United Kingdom.

They may be willing to talk about their clothes and explain any special significance of particular articles and to introduce different musical instruments and explain their place in the community. Likewise, involve those with knowledge of particular disabilities and abilities.

- If you are creating a particular background for a Persona Doll, involve the families with the same cultural background so that the children are not given wrong information. If families are not able to do this, approach the various community groups for help.

Additional stories

Barkow, H. (2001) *That's My Mum,* London: Mantra Lingua. (Mia and Kai have dual heritage, and they get fed up with people assuming that their mothers are childminders and find a way of solving their problem. Available in English and more than twenty bilingual editions.)

Benjamin, F. (2007) *My Two Grannies,* London: Frances Lincoln. (Alvina has two grannies: one comes from Trinidad, the other from the north of England. They dress, eat and play differently, and when they come to look after Alvina, it makes for difficulties at first, until Alvina comes up with a way to respect everyone's way of doing things.)

Boswell, G. (2002) *Rauni and the Rye,* Newland: Lincolnshire Traveller Education Service. (Story of a Romany family and their dogs. Dual language in Romany and English.)

Cunningham, K. (2004) *Jel Akai Chavvies,* Trumpington: Cambridge-shire Race Equality and Diversity Service. (A nursery-rhyme book focusing on travellers.)

Daly, N. (2000) *Jamela's Dress,* London: Frances Lincoln. (Set in a South African town, Jamela has some fun with the material for Thelma's wedding dress, but things go wrong and Mum is very upset, but a solution is found just in time for the big day.)

Damon, E. (2003) *All Kinds of Beliefs,* London: Mantra Lingua. (This lift-the-flap book celebrates the beliefs of all kinds of children in a warm and straightforward way. Available in English and a few bilingual editions.)

—— (2005) *What is Peace?* London: Mantra Lingua. (A dual-language flap book that introduces the concept of peace to very young children. Available in English and more than fifteen bilingual editions.)

Fraser, S. (2005) *Grandma's Saturday Soup,* London: Mantra Lingua. (Mimi misses her Jamaican grandma with her special Saturday Soup and her wonderful stories that conjure up many images of life in Jamaica. Available in English and more than twenty bilingual editions.)

Gower, C. (2005) *Long-Long's New Year,* London: Frances Lincoln. (A snapshot of life in contemporary China as Long-Long accompanies his grandfather to market for the first time to sell their cabbages so they can buy food and decorations for the New Year celebrations.)

Grindley, S. (2005) *Home for Christmas,* London: Frances Lincoln. (A homeless boy wonders what it would like to have a warm and loving family, then in the night he is woken by a bright light and the crying of a baby. The story of the birth of baby Jesus. For children aged five to eight years.)

Hertfordshire Traveller Education Project (1999) *Monday Morning,* Hertford: Hertfordshire TEP. (A short-story book with a traveller perspective focusing on three children from different homes and cultures as they get ready for their first day at a new school.)

Hest, A. (1996) *Baby Duck and the Bad Eyeglasses,* London: Walker Books. (Baby Duck does not think her new eyeglasses look right. In the park, she hides behind a tree, but Grandpa is able to cheer her up.)

Hoffman, M. (2007) *An Angel Just Like Me,* London: Frances Lincoln. (Concerned that there are no black angels, Tyler searches in all the shops but to no avail, but on Christmas Day a surprise delivery convinces him that there are angels just like him.)

—— (2007) *Princess Grace,* London: Frances Lincoln. (Grace and her friends challenge the stereotype of a princess, who dresses in pink and wears a crown, and in the school parade dress up as princesses from around the world.)

Jones, S. L. (2006) *Little One We Knew You'd Come,* London: Frances Lincoln. (The birth of a much-waited-for baby is linked to the story of the birth of Jesus. A beautifully illustrated, evocative book.)

Koralek, J. (2005) *The Moses Basket,* London: Frances Lincoln. (The story of how Baby Moses was saved from Pharaoh's soldiers because his mother hid him in a basket amongst the bulrushes at the edge of the river. Here he was discovered by Pharaoh's daughter, and his own mother got to nurse him.)

MacKinnon, D. and Martin, A. (2006) *Away in a Manger,* London: Frances Lincoln. (Young children prepare for a nativity play that delights everyone. The book contains simple instructions for making the costumes.)

Petty, K. (2006) *Playtime,* London: Frances Lincoln. (Pictures of children from around the world playing their favourite games, alone or with their friends. It was created in collaboration with Oxfam.)

Pfister, M. (1995) *Rainbow Fish to the Rescue,* Zurich: North-South Book Inc. (A lonely striped fish cannot join in a game of tag with Rainbow Fish and his friends because he doesn't have shiny scales, but when he is in danger from a shark, Rainbow Fish has to decide between his new friends and the striped fish.)

Robert, N. B. (2005) *Welcome to the World Baby,* London: Mantra Lingua. (The arrival of a new baby sister for Tariq leads to children from different cultural backgrounds showing one thing to do with their senses that is special at the time of a new birth in their house, and sharing it with the other children. At the end of the story, they have a very special visitor. Available in English and more than twenty-five bilingual editions.)

Shanahan, L. (2006) *The Postman's Dog,* London: Frances Lincoln. (Charlie the postman loves delivering letters to lonely people and always has time for a chat and to pat their dogs. One day he feels very lonely himself and is encouraged by the people on his round to get a dog to give him hugs and licks.)

Thomas, P. (2003) *The Skin I'm In,* London: Hodder Wayland. (Gives examples of racist behaviour and teaches about the acceptance of different cultures and lifestyles. For children aged four to eight years.)

Persona Doll story

Introduce the Persona Doll over a number of sessions before talking about an issue.

Meet Hyunji

Kim Hyunji is nearly four years old. Sometimes people call her Kim, but that is her last name. In South Korea where her family have come from, the family name is written first. (*Can you tell us all your names? Do you have a different name at home?*)

She lives with her mummy and daddy, her big brother Seokjun, who is eight years old, and her baby sister Eunjoo, who is six months old. (*Who is in your family?*) Seokjun and Hyunji were born in the biggest city in South Korea called Seoul, but Eunjoo was born in a hospital in England. The family live in a rented flat while Daddy is studying at the University of Surrey. (*Does anyone else live in a flat? Are there lots of steps, or do you have a lift?*) They will be in England for two more years. Hyunji likes the flat but is sad that they have no garden to play in. One good thing is that it is very close to Richmond Park, and they go for a walk there nearly every day. Hyunji loves to see the deer, and sometimes she takes some bread to feed to them. The deer come really close and put their wet noses in her hand. Hyunji would like to have a pet, but that is not allowed in the flats. (*Have you any pets at home? What are they called? What do they like to do?*)

Seokjun goes to school, and he speaks Korean and English very well now. Mummy and Daddy speak Korean and English and can read Mandarin letters like people who live in China. They all speak Korean at home, because

Hyunji

Mummy and Daddy say they will soon be going back home and the children will need to speak both languages for school.

Hyunji's family eat a lot of rice at home with soup that sometimes has
chicken, beef or pork in as well as vegetables. Sometimes on Sundays they
go to a Korean restaurant, but on the children's birthdays they choose to go
to MacDonald's or Pizza Hut. They have this food in their country as well,
but Mummy says it is not healthy to have too many chips. Hyunji still thinks
they taste really good. Her favourite fruit is Korean pears. They look different
to English pears. They are round with a yellow skin, and Hyunji thinks they

are delicious. She says she will bring some next time she comes, so you can taste them.

Hyunji goes to nursery in England. She was very frightened on the first day, but now she has lots of friends and is sorry that she cannot go on Saturday and Sunday as well. (*What did you feel like on your first day? Did you feel worried or anxious? Were you excited as well? Did anyone help you? Did you find it hard to make friends?*) Seokjun went to school for a year before they came to England. He said it was very different: the children all sat in rows and answered questions. It was rude to look in your teacher's eyes, but he said in this school, his teacher likes him to ask questions and to look at her when she is talking. He is getting better at this but still feels a bit uncomfortable about it. None of the teachers at school can speak Korean, but Seokjun says there are a group of children in his class who are Korean, and the teacher sometimes puts them together, so they can talk about their lesson in Korean. Afterwards, one of the children tells the teacher and the other children, in English, what they have said. At other times, they work with the English children so they can learn the language. Seokjun has a special partner called James, who is good at reading and can explain things very well. Seokjun likes to sit next to James, and he is going to invite him to come to his house after school one day.

Hyunji's family are Buddhists, although in Korea her friend next door was a Christian and her family went to church on Sundays. But they all enjoyed the big festivals. Hyunji loves Christmas; she thinks it is nearly as good as the Lotus Lantern Festival they have every year around the end of May. They have lots of people dressing up in fancy costumes and dancing in the streets and lots of music. It is very exciting. Another good time is the New Year when everyone puts on their best clothes and cooks special food. Hyunji's grandma and aunties and uncles and all their children and friends come round to visit, and everyone is happy. In the morning, all the family walk up the hill to Hyunji's grandad's grave and say some prayers and put burning sticks in the ground that make a funny smell and put some money on the grave and burn it. Mummy says it is for Grandad to spend in his new life. Hyunji hopes that she can go to see him soon in his new place, but Mummy says it will be a long time until she can go, but she will go one day. Hyunji's teacher has asked Mummy if she will go into school next time it is the New Year festival and do some cooking with the children and tell them about their Korean celebrations. Hyunji feels a bit shy about this, but she says she will help her mummy and she wants to show her the beautiful Chinese dragon they are making. She wants to take her favourite CD of drums and gongs for the children to hear, and the teacher says they can use it for the dragon dance. Hyunji can't wait to tell you all about it. (*Have you ever made a dragon for Chinese New Year? Have you ever beat a drum or a gong? What does it sound like?*)

⬡⬡⬡ The EYFS principles

The EYFS principles are grouped into four themes which are concerned with the individual needs of the child, the importance of building positive relationships and the need for the adults in the setting to create an environment that enables the child to learn and to develop to the best of their ability. As these themes relate to this section on sense of community, the focus is on how the children understand and respect their own needs, views, cultures and beliefs and those of other people. The children need to be given the opportunities to develop as people in their own right with their own feelings and developing opinions, but from within the nurturing care of their family and the community. As they become increasingly aware of their own needs, they will also become more aware of the culture of their own family and those of the communities to which they belong. How they are dressed and the way they are fed and cared for will be according to certain cultural norms. However, these will only make up the visible part of their culture, the tip of the iceberg. Below the surface will be attitudes to such weighty matters as gender roles, skin tone, disability, modesty, respect, beliefs, discipline, birth, death, marriage, divorce, education, as well as views on simpler matters such as keeping pets. Such views will be subsumed by young children unconsciously. These will be the things that give them a sense of belonging in the early years. Many of these attitudes will be shared by the practitioners in the setting, but others will not. Of those, some will equate to a different way of doing things, and in these cases the views of the parents and carers must be respected and ways found to accommodate their wishes. However, where the children have picked up messages at home that lead them to act in discriminatory ways, then this must be challenged by the practitioners and, likewise, by the parents and carers if any members of staff are acting in a biased way in the setting. If such attitudes are allowed to flourish unchecked, then it will impossible for the children to form positive relationships with others. Mutual respect is a necessary foundation for the children if they are to learn to take account of the feelings of others in their decision-making and to take responsibility for their own actions. Providing the children with an equal opportunity is not the same as treating them the same because their needs are different. We all belong to communities of one kind or another and yet we are all unique. Helping the children to celebrate their similarities and their differences will go a long way to enabling them to become responsible human beings in whatever communities they find themselves in the future.

Further recommended reading

Ainscow, M., Conteh, J., Dyson, A. and Gallanaugh, F. (2007) *Children in Primary Education: Demography, Culture, Diversity and Inclusion.* Cambridge: University of Cambridge, Faculty of Education, Primary Review Research Survey 5/1. Available online at www.primaryreview.org.uk/Downloads/Int_ Reps/4.Children_development-learning/Primary_Review_5–1_briefing_Demo graphy-culture-diversity-inclusion_071214.pdf (accessed 2 July 2008).

Brightwell, J. and Fidgin, N. (2005) *To Begin at the Beginning: Bringing a Global Dimension to the Early Years,* Poole: Development Education in Dorset.

Broadhead, P. (2004) *Early Years Play and Learning: Developing Social Skills and Co-operation,* London: RoutledgeFalmer.

Collins, M. (2005) *It's OK to be Sad,* London: Paul Chapman.

—— (2007) *Circle Time for the Very Young,* 2nd edn, London: Paul Chapman.

Crawley, H. (2006) *Eating Well for Under-5s in Child Care: Nutritional and Practical Guidelines,* 2nd edn, Abbots Langley: The Caroline Walker Trust.

Featherstone, S. (ed.) (2005) *The Little Book of Circle Time,* London: Featherstone Educational.

Garforth, H., Hopper, L., Lowe, B. and Robinson, L. (2006) *Growing Up Global: Early Years Global Education Handbook,* Reading: Reading International Solidarity Centre.

Hyson, M. (2004) *The Emotional Development of Young Children: Building an Emotion-Centred Curriculum,* 2nd edn, New York: Teachers College, Columbia University.

Lynch, E. W. and Hansen, M. J. (1998) *Developing Cross-Cultural Competence: A Guide for Working with Children and Families,* Baltimore, Md.: Paul H. Brookes.

Mort, L. (2004) *Circle Time: 10-Minute Ideas for the Early Years,* London: Scholastic.

Mosley, J. (2005) *Circle Time for Young Children,* London: RoutledgeFalmer.

Plummer, D. M. (2005) *The Adventures of the Little Tin Tortoise: A Self-Esteem Story with Activities for Teachers, Parents and Carers,* London: Jessica Kingsley.

—— (2006) *Self-Esteem Games for Children,* London: Jessica Kingsley.

Rawstrone, A. (2007) 'Be honest' (Positive relationships series: Telling lies), *Nursery World,* December. Available online at www.nurseryworld.co.uk/news/login/773441 (accessed 2 July 2008).

Rogers, B. and McPherson, E. (2008) *Behaviour Management With Young Children: Crucial First Steps With Children 3–7 Years,* London: Sage.

Siraj-Blatchford, I. and Clarke, P. (2000) *Supporting Identity, Diversity and Language in the Early Years,* Buckingham: Open University Press.

Sunderland, M. (2001) *Using Story Telling as a Therapeutic Tool with Children,* Milton Keynes: Speechmark.

White, M. (2007) *Magic Circles: Building Self-Esteem through Circle Time,* 2nd edn, London: Lucky Duck.

Useful websites

www.communityinsight.co.uk (Community Insight specialises in inclusive, non-stereotyped material for practitioners and for children.)

www.forestbooks.com (Forest Bookshop specialise in books and resources on deafness.)

www.letterboxlibrary.com (Letterbox Library specialises in inclusive, non-stereotyped material for children.)

www.mantralingua.com (Mantra posters include a number of different languages as well as English: Ourselves features children involved in various activities with the caption 'I can feel happy, sad, hear, see, smell, touch, taste, jump, dance and cartwheel' (30 centimetres × 160 centimetres). They also produce dual-language books.)

www.multiculturalbooks.info (Multicultural Book Services in Bradford provides a wide range of material to support children of all ages living in our multilingual, multi-faith society, and their teachers.)

www.puppetsbypost.com (*Puppets by Post* have a large selection of finger, glove, rod-arm and large body puppets at reasonable prices.)

www.stickykids.co.uk (The Sticky Kids collection produces educational music and movement for the under-sevens. The CDs help to raise the children's levels of confidence and encourage them to express a range of emotions.)

www.festivalshop.co.uk (The Festival Shop produces a very useful catalogue of multi-faith, multicultural and citizenship resources.)